HOLLOW CITY

A Haymarket Book

HOLLOW CITY

The Siege of San Francisco and the Crisis of American Urbanism

◆

REBECCA SOLNIT

Text

SUSAN SCHWARTZENBERG

Photographs

London • New York

First published by Verso 2000
Text © 2000 Rebecca Solnit
Images © 2000 Susan Schwartzenberg
and the individual artists

Verso

UK: 6 Meard Street, London W1V 3HR

USA: 180 Varick Street, New York, NY 10014-4606

Verso is the imprint of New Left Books

ISBN   1 85984 794 3

British Library Cataloguing in Publication Data
A catalogue record for this book is available from the British Library

Library of Congress Cataloging-in-Publication Data
A catalog record for this book is available from the Library of Congress

Designed by Steven Hiatt and Susan Schwartzenberg
Typeset by Steven Hiatt, San Francisco, California
Printed and bound in Great Britain by The Bath Press Limited, Bath, England

Contents

dedicated to the artists and activists born in 2000

and

in memory of Frances Solnit Gallegos
East Los Angeles, July 31, 1937–Sonoma County, March 24, 2000
bohemian, saboteur of bulldozers, supplier of books,
excellent aunt

A rising tide lifts all boats—
and if you don't have a boat, you're fucked.
— Bob, an activist for the homeless
giving a tour of gentrified downtown Seattle

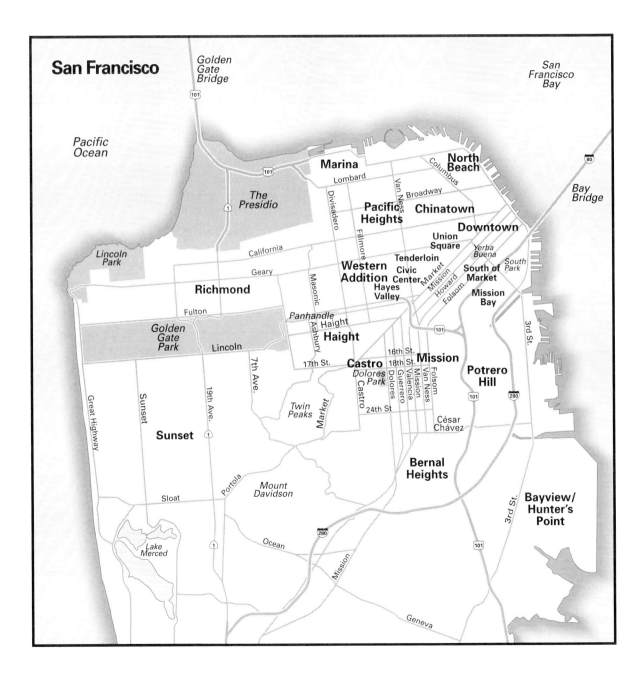

This book was conceived and carried out as a collaboration between writer Rebecca Solnit and artist Susan Schwartzenberg. Solnit wrote the text first, and Schwartzenberg put together the visual material afterwards, though our conversation about the transformation of San Francisco extended through both processes and impacted the results in both cases. Though Schwartzenberg often chose to use work by other artists, the visuals as a whole are entirely her creation, a feat of coordination and research as well as photography. *Hollow City* was carried out with considerable speed and the hope that the occasional roughnesses would be compensated for by timeliness: it is a report from the front lines, not a post-mortem.

Wrecking-Ball Overture

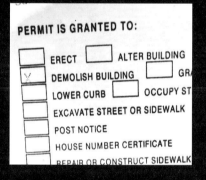

Demolition of a housing project, Hayes Valley

Demolition of an office complex, Mission Street near First Street

Formerly Clear Café and May's Cleaners, Polk and Turk Streets, 2000

This whole city is a construction zone.

I came from Phoenix. I can't afford to live here,
so I'm sleeping on the floor at a friend's house.
I came because there is so much work.
There are a lot of guys like me on the job.
— *Construction worker*

Moscone West Convention Center, Howard and Fourth Streets

These get built all over the town, and most are sold before they're finished being built. I just paint, day after day—always white. Yeah, we build them, but we won't ever make enough money to buy one.

– *Interior painter*

Loft condo, Folsom and Seventh

There's so much work right now and not enough qualified people to do it. Some days I feel like my head is about to explode—the intensity, the pace, the stress are just so great. It's all market-driven and client-controlled. When I first came here I had any number of great offers and I'm someone who remembers the slow times only too well. Some people where I work routinely put in 40 to 50 percent in overtime hours. We're professionals, so we don't get paid for it. Most of us probably can't even afford to live in the buildings we're designing.

– *Architect*

"Who are you photographing for?"

"Just me."

"You're not working
for an insurance
company are you?
I'm not getting
sued, am I?"

"No. Why would you
be getting sued?"

"I don't know. You try
to build housing
in this city and they sue you."

"What are you building here?"

"Condos—higher end."
                    — *Conversation with a developer*

There are too many projects happening at the same time and none of them are managed in any sensible way. No one has time, or cares to pay attention to the details—we do, but we lose money because we care. It's pure greed—everyone wants to develop as much as they can and make as much money as possible. It's crazy.

–Landscape architect

Gas station at the edge of South Park and Fourth Street

Architect's office

Condiment City, 2000.

The St. John Coltrane congregation's ceremonial march to a temporary site after their eviction.

San Francisco, Capital of the Twenty-First Century

Saturday night a new bar called Fly opens on Divisadero Street and immediately becomes a mecca for white kids. Sunday evening the St. John Coltrane African Orthodox Church a few blocks down the boulevard holds a benefit to help it relocate from its home of twenty-nine years. And this bar and this church aren't even in the San Francisco neighborhoods that are being most rapidly changed. What's happening on Divisadero Street in the Western Addition is just the spillover from the wild mutation of the Mission District, once a bastion of Latino culture and cheap housing, and of the formerly industrial South of Market, districts that are becoming the global capital of the Internet economy.

San Francisco has been for most of its 150-year existence both a refuge and an anomaly. Soon it will be neither. Gentrification is transforming the city by driving out the poor and working class, including those who have chosen to give their lives over to unlucrative pursuits such as art, activism, social experimentation, social service. But gentrification is just the fin above water. Below is the rest of the shark: a new American economy in which most of us will be poorer, a few will be far richer, and everything will be faster, more homogenous and more controlled or controllable. The technology boom and the accompanying housing crisis have fast-forwarded San Francisco into the newest version of the American future, a version that also is being realized in Boston, Seattle, and other cities from New York and Atlanta to Denver and Portland.

A decade ago Los Angeles looked like the future—urban decay, open warfare, segregation, despair, injustice and corruption—but the new future looks like San Francisco: a frenzy of financial speculation, covert coercions, overt erasures, a barrage of novelty-item restaurants, websites, technologies and trends, the despair of unemployment replaced by the numbness of incessant work hours and the anxiety of destabilized jobs, homes and neighborhoods. Thirty-five percent of the venture capital in this country is in the Bay Area, along with 30 percent of the multimedia/ Internet businesses, and the boom that started in Silicon Valley has produced a ripple effect throughout the region from south of San Jose to Napa and Sonoma in the north.[1] San Francisco has had the most expensive housing of any major American city in the nation for two decades, but in the past few years housing prices—both sales and rents—have been skyrocketing, along with commercial rents. New businesses are coming in at a hectic pace, and they in turn generate new boutiques, restaurants and bars that displace earlier businesses, particularly nonprofits, and the new industry's workers have been outbidding for rentals and buying houses out from under tenants at a breakneck pace. Regionally, home sale and rental prices have gone up by 30 percent over the past three years, but the rate of increase is far more dramatic in San Francisco (where rents rose 37 percent from 1996 to 1997, before the boom really hit, and nowadays can go up 20 percent in less than six months in some neighborhoods, vacancy rates are below 1 percent, and houses routinely sell for a hundred thousand dollars over offering price).[2]

Part of the cause is the 70,000 or so jobs created in the Bay Area annually, nearly half a million since 1995.[3] Evictions have skyrocketed to make way for the new workers and profiteers of the new industries; at last estimate there were seven official evictions a day in San Francisco, and 70 percent of those evicted leave the city.[4] For decades San Francisco has been retooling itself to make tourism its primary industry, but in late 1998 a city survey found nearly as many people were employed in the brand-new Internet/multimedia industry as in the old hotel industry, 17,600 compared to 19,200, and that doesn't count the huge number of freelancers working in multimedia who bring the numbers to more than 50,000 (in a city whose population is about 800,000).[5] Construction and business ser-

Brian Goggin, Defenestration Building, Sixth and Howard Streets (public artwork of furniture leaping from the windows of a condemned building on Skid Row, with murals on ground level).

vices to accommodate this boom have also expanded rapidly, though the construction workers are not building housing they themselves are likely to be able to inhabit. All over the city, buildings are being torn down and replaced with bigger ones, long-vacant lots are being filled in, condos built and sold, old industrial buildings and former nonprofit offices turned into dot-com offices and upscale lofts. As San Francisco's Urban Habitat Program puts it, "The growing gap between low wage and high wage workers and the scarcity of housing, especially affordable housing for low income households, is resulting in the displacement of low income people by middle and high income households in historically urban communities of color."[6] San Francisco and many Silicon Valley cities are exacerbating this housing crisis by encouraging the influx of new enterprises and new jobs without addressing the housing needs such jobs create, thereby ensuring a brutal free-market struggle for places to live and an aggravation of traffic problems that are already among the worst in the nation.

Silicon Valley was the sprawling suburban capital of the first wave of new technology—computers, electronics and software design. In recent years San Francisco has become both a bedroom community for the Valley's highly paid workers and the capital of the next technological wave—the Internet, aka multimedia, with biotechnology about to become a huge presence in Mission Bay. The newness of this new technology is celebrated everywhere, but in some ways it's just continuing by other means an old history in San Francisco: an assault on the poor that began with urban renewal programs in the 1950s and has taken many forms since. And in some ways, the new technology is returning us to an old era, perhaps to the peak years of the Industrial Revolution, with huge gaps between rich and poor, endless work hours and a spartan work ethic, a devout faith in progress and technology. The manic greed at work here also recalls the Gold Rush, another nineteenth-century phenomenon often referenced in the Bay Area; but the differences matter, too. In 1849, California was a remote outpost and prices on everything soared when the world rushed in: laundresses and farmers could charge prices in proportion to the wealth being dug out of the Motherlode and join the boom, a prospect impossible in globalized contemporary California.

The influx of high-tech money is producing a sort of "resort economy" in the Bay Area, with real estate prices so inflated that the people whose work holds the place together can't afford to live in it. In Jackson Hole, Wyoming, the latte-makers and janitors live on the other side of a mountain pass that becomes treacherous in winter; in the Bay Area, the help just faces an increasingly long and hard commute, and air pollution has increased with the sprawl accommodating those who can't live in the most expensive real estate in the country. What Jeff Goodell wrote about the economy of Silicon Valley is coming true here: "The brutality of the Silicon Valley economy is apparent not just to newcomers who arrive here to seek their fortunes but also to anyone who is so unwise as to choose a field of work for love, not money. Schoolteachers, cops, construction workers, nurses, even doctors and lawyers—as the tide of wealth rises around them, many are finding it harder to stay afloat. Despite the utopian rhetoric of Silicon Valley boosters … it's clear that Silicon Valley is developing into a two-tier society: those who have caught the technological wave and those who are being left behind. This is not simply a phenomenon of class or race or age or the distribution of wealth—although those are all important factors. It's really about the Darwinian nature of unfettered capitalism when it's operating at warp speed. And while the divide between the haves and have-nots may be more extreme in Silicon Valley than in other parts of the country right now, that won't last long. 'Silicon Valley-style economies are what we can look forward to everywhere,' says Robert H. Frank, an economist at Cornell University who has

St. John Coltrane Church procession on Turk Street.

long studied the increasing gap between the rich and poor. 'In this new economy, either you have a lottery ticket or you don't. And the people who don't are not happy about it.'"[7]

When the new economy arrived in San Francisco, it began to lay waste the city's existing culture—culture both in the sense of cultural diversity, as in ethnic cultures, and of creative activity, artistic and political. Both are under siege, and while the racial aspects of gentrification and urban renewal have often been addressed, this book focuses particularly on creative activity (and, of course, the two are extensively overlapping sets—hip-hop and mural movements being two hallowed examples). Cities are both the administrative hub from which order, control and hierarchy emanate and, traditionally, the place where that order is subverted. This subversion comes from the free space of the city in which people and ideas circulate, and bohemia is most significant as the freest part of the free city, a place where the poor, the radical, the marginal and the creative over-lap. Bohemia is not so much a population as a condition, a condition of urbanism where the young go to invent themselves and from which cultural innovation and insurrection arise. As that cultural space contracts, the poor and individual artists will go elsewhere, but bohemia may well go away altogether, here and in cities across the country.

Artmaking has been, at least since bohemia and modernism appeared in nineteenth-century Paris, largely an urban enterprise: the closer to museums, publishers, audiences, patrons, politicians, other enemies and each other, the better for artists and for art. For if cities have been essential to artists, artists have been essential to cities. This complex gave rise to the definitive modernisms of the Left Bank, Montmartre and Greenwich Village. Being an artist was one way of being a participant in the debate about meaning and value, and the closer to the center of things one is the more one can participate. This is part of what makes an urbanity worth celebrating, this braiding together of disparate lives, but the new gentrification threatens to yank out some of the strands altogether, diminishing urbanism itself. Perhaps the new urbanism will result in old cities that function like suburbs as those who were suburbia's blandly privileged take them over. In the postwar years, the white middle class fled cities, which created the crises of abandonment, scarce city revenue, and depression that defined urban trouble through the 1970s, but the poor and the bohemian who stuck to cities often made something lively there anyway; now those who once fled have come back and created an unanticipated crisis of wealth for those raised on the urban crisis of poverty. Wealth has proven able to ravage cities as well as or better than poverty.

In discussions about gentrification here, artists are a controversial subject—sometimes because the focus on the displacement of artists eclipses the displacement of the less privileged in general, sometimes because art-

Eviction Defense Network poster, Mission District, 1999, with graphic by Eric Drooker.

ists have played roles in promoting gentrification as well as resisting it, sometimes because artists and their ilk are conceived of as middle-class people slumming and playing poor. After all, modern bohemians are often people who were born among the middle class but who chose to live among the poor, while some artists socialize with and service the rich. For the time being, remember that *painter* means both those who have covered the Mission District with murals celebrating radical history and those who sell in downtown galleries (and that some of those in the downtown galleries, like Enrique Chagoya, are making paintings too incendiary to be publicly sponsored murals). And for this book, *bohemian* refers to all the participants in the undivided spectrum of radical politics and artistic culture here, a spectrum that includes Marxists who look down on culture and artists who don't notice politics until it evicts them, as well as a lively community of innovative activists and political cultures, or rather dozens of such communities. Whether it was Allen Ginsberg decrying "Moloch whose mind is pure machinery! Moloch whose blood is running money!" in the first reading of *Howl* in 1955 or the Sierra Club in the early 1960s lobbying for wilderness preservation with lavish photographic books, art and politics have been all tangled up together here for a long time.

Artists, however, are just bit-players in a major transformation of cities. Those who really orchestrate urban development have another agenda altogether. Neil Smith and Peter Williams summed it up in 1986: "The direction of change is toward a new central city dominated by middle-class residential areas, a concentration of professional, administrative, and managerial employment, the upmarket recreation and entertainment facilities that cater to this population (as well as to tourists).... The moment of the present restructuring is toward a more peripheralized working class, in geographical terms."[8] This is the context behind multimedia replacing meatpacking in the South of Market, Fly arriving as the Coltrane church departs in my own Western Addition neighborhood, and valet parking suddenly appearing where lowriders once cruised Mission Street. As for the effects of this gentrification, what is happening in San Francisco is happening everywhere, which is precisely the problem (and because the term *gentrification* traditionally describes the transformation of a neighborhood rather than a whole city or region, it may be an inadequate term altogether for this awful upgrading). What Bill Saunders, editor of *Harvard Design Magazine*, writes of the changes in Harvard Square could describe this city and many others: "The new Square reflects the world-wide increase in the imperialism of a small, delocalized number of rich and powerful organizations. . . . The Square is now: more impersonal (e.g., the sales and service people are rarely familiar or interested in the buyer), more expensive (after inflation), more exclusionary (less welcoming and less affordable to eccentrics, the middle and working classes, and the marginally employed), more predictable, more uniform, and more like other places (a Gap is a Gap is a Gap). . . . Along with the Square's greater polish, luxury and upscale taste come new subtle pressures to be rich and beautiful, constrained and role-bound. The new red brick architecture—often replacing low, tippy, wood-frame buildings—is decorous and solid but boring. One longs for more bad taste, for more surprise, dirt, and looseness, more anarchic, unself-conscious play. . . . I think of appealing college towns as at least somewhat Bohemian. That word now applies to nothing in the square."[9]

One Friday night a few weeks after Fly opened, I go there with a friend and look at the crowd mingling with the utter absorbedness of the very young. Clean-cut but aspiring to be cool, the women in very tight and the men in very loose clothes drink big glasses of beer and saki cocktails. The front half of the bar has expensive chairs and frosted red glass light sconces, but in the back, along with a purple pool table and thrift-store couches and chairs, is a mural on shiny purple paint featuring elongated females of various skin colors in skimpy seventies clothes waving their tubular limbs. It's clearly meant to evoke a fantasy of the area and of an era, a sort of bell-bottomed floating world without strife or tension. The name Fly, written in seventies-style fat round red letters on the illuminated plastic sign outside, evidently refers to the 1970s blaxsploitation *Superfly* films that film director Quentin Tarantino appropriated, a funny reference for a predominantly white kid's bar in a formerly African-American neighborhood. (A scruffy musician in the neighborhood tells me that Fly claimed "last call" had been called when he went to Fly for a midnight beer, only to find that the well-dressed couple who came in after him was being served.) Fly is across the street from a neighborhood fixture, Eddie's Cafe, a decades-old soul-food restaurant, with a more recently arrived Asian-owned liquor-grocery store and an Arab-owned cafe on the other corners. It's far posher than the other businesses at this intersection, and its mural is a fantasy substituted for history—a fantasy because it proposes a fictional history based on entertainment, while it participates in erasing the real history of a neighborhood wracked first by urban renewal, then by crack and gentrification. The jarring thing about these privileged young newcomers is that they accept as unquestioned fact what those who were there before them know as deterioration, outrage, erasure, distortion of what came before. The new San Francisco is run for the dot-com workers, multimedia executives and financiers of the new boom, and memory is one of the things that is being lost in the rapid turnover and all-out exile of tenants, organizations, nonchain businesses and even communities.

The storefront Church of St. John Coltrane exemplifies culture in every sense: it's religious, artistic, ethnic, political and social at the same time. It feeds the poor three times a week and serves as one of the last remaining links to the golden age of the Fillmore District before it was gutted by urban renewal. And as an eccentric, individualist cultural hybrid—making free jazz a sacrament—it represents what has always made San Francisco distinctive, while Fly is a commercial enterprise that could be anywhere people old enough to drink and affluent enough to appreciate hip light fixtures congregate. You could say it's not fair to compare a bar and a church, but the neighborhood's African-American bars all vanished long ago—though the former jazz club midway between Fly and St. John's has become the Justice League, a hip-hop club, and nearby Storyville caters to a mixed crowd of young jazz aficionados. Both bar and church postulate a relationship to African-American cultural history—to jazz and spirituality at the one, to fashion and movies in the other. It may be unkind to single Fly out, but it signifies the new order as neatly as the church signifies the old. Last year a new owner bought the building whose ground-floor storefront the church has inhabited for so long and doubled the church's rent, a de facto eviction. Probably, like a lot of new landlords who've paid enormous prices for San Francisco real estate, he needs a better return on his investment than St. John Coltrane can provide.

The Sunday after my excursion to Fly, I take my bike the few blocks from my home of nearly two decades to the Coltrane church. It's the first sunny spring morning after a lot of rain, and people seem rejuvenated. There are some others out there waiting with me for the 10 o'clock service, and I read the program for an older man in a tweedy suit who's getting his glasses out and we begin to talk. He's lived here half a century and first got into politics here working for Helen Gahagan Douglas, the woman who ran for the Senate against Richard Nixon in 1950. He's one of the more progressive forces on the Democratic Central Committee, judging by what he says about gentrification and Mayor Willie Brown, and he's come here to see what can be done to keep the church in its present loca-

tion. A couple of shaggy young men sit on the curb. A couple shows up, then another man. At 10:15 Bishop Franzo King drives by and his daughters and Sister Deborah, a sturdy, radiant woman with a kerchief over her dreadlocks, get out. As Sister Deborah puts a key in the storefront door, a young white guy in black hipster sunglasses and a stocking cap shaped vaguely like a fez opens up from inside, and we all shuffle in. There's a good stereo system on which Coltrane plays while the white guy in the glasses sings softly and one of the daughters hums along. The church's right wall is lined with glossy paintings on some kind of board, like giant playing cards, portraying figures in the Eastern Orthodox and Byzantine sensibility of flattened, large-eyed, stiff and highly stylized figures. They're beautifully painted, and in them all the angels, saints and the Madonna and child have dark skin. The left wall features clippings and the text of Coltrane's "A Love Supreme." Off by itself is a smaller painting of Coltrane himself in Byzantine-icon style, with delicate flames lined up like a graduating class inside the mouth of his saxophone. A row of fluorescent lights illuminate these and the altar that's off-center in the back of this unremodeled storefront. Front and center on the altar is a portrait of Jesus with neat dreadlocks.

Bishop King has put on what looks like a red yarmulke, the six battered wooden pews have become half-full, and the service begins with the recitation of the Lord's Prayer and other prayers in a formal style. But after the prayers, he begins to preach like the African-American Baptists and Methodists in the neighborhood, fervently, rhythmically, with antiphony supplied by Sister Deborah's rich voice in the back and the two young women up front clapping hands. The pale hipster in the dark glasses takes up a tambourine and beats it above his head. Some of the people in the pews are swaying to the sounds. Bishop King's prayers ask God to soften the hearts of those up high and to care for the needy below, and he says that Heaven is the true home of this church that is becoming homeless. Sister Deborah comes forward to sing with a cordless mike, and Bishop King gets behind the red drum set next to her and drums away with the same stateliness he preaches with. Turning sideways, I see that a young Asian couple has come in and we've got all the races represented, if the guy with the soul patch is as Hispanic as he looks. "The strongest argument for San Francisco over, say, Dallas (other than weather and natural elements like hills and oceans)," my friend Catherine e-mails me from the Mission District that day, "is that here people still mix."

I skip out on bible class to bicycle through Golden Gate Park, which begins a few blocks west of the church, and I pass groups of martial artists training, elderly Chinese doing tai chi, slack-faced men in cars waiting to be solicited for adventures in the shrubbery, scrambling small children and bounding dogs on the lawns, rollerbladers dancing to a boombox, homeless people sunning themselves and what looks to be a matador class with three students and an instructor (but no bull) waving hot pink capes. On my way back from a view of the Pacific, I stop at the park's M. H. de Young Memorial Museum and admire the way the Portuguese émigré artist Rigo has turned his space in a group show of Bay Area artists into a mini-museum of American Indian Movement leader Leonard Peltier. Rigo's installation includes a display of Peltier's laboriously realistic paintings of indigenous people, a facsimile of his jail cell, and a series of footsteps, one for each year of Peltier's long incarceration on dubious charges. In other galleries of the museum paintings, prints and photographs dating back to the nineteenth century depict the city's history.

I come home from the park to a phone message from the performance artist Guillermo Gómez-Peña. When I call him back, he tells me of several incidents in which Latinos were attacked or thrown out of bars in a Mission District that no longer feels like their home. "It is horrible, horrible, horrible," he says with emotion, and he repeats what several others have told me, that the San Francisco police are busting the neighborhood's Latino bars for every possible code infraction, thereby accelerating their turnover into enterprises catering to wealthier and whiter new arrivals. The Mission is named after Mission Dolores, the church built by Franciscan missionaries in the eighteenth century, and it has had a Latino presence ever since, notably since the 1930s, but that population is under siege—mostly by money. Guillermo tells me that twenty of his friends in the Mission have already left, and the community he came to be part of five years ago may not exist much longer.

A triple wave of real estate rapaciousness is evicting people from their homes, putting nonprofits and small enterprises out of business or out of town, and bringing in hordes of chain stores that are erasing the distinctness and the memory of San Francisco, but for days after my conversation with Guillermo the news seems to come in pairs. In the *New Mission News,* on the left side: "Mission Armory Developer Says He Wants to Do the Right Thing"—a fortress vacant for decades in one of the bleaker parts of the North Mission, once proposed as a homeless shelter, is now slated to become a dot-com worksite. On the right side, "Proposed Resource Center for the Homeless Is Now Homeless." And in the *San Francisco Independent* there's a double pairing: on the front page of the Neighborhood Section, "Street Tree Planting Programs in Budget Peril" and "Planners OK Pottery Barn for Market and Castro" with the subhead "Neighborhood Divided over Chain

Store." These stories jump to the back page, where the left side has a new story, "Popular Richmond [District] Dance Studio Faces Eviction," with an aside that dance studios all over the city are losing their spaces. A week later, the *Chronicle* runs a gossip item on "startup billionaire Marc Greenberg," his twenty-million-dollar house, his half-million-dollar bachelor party and the million he paid Elton John to play at the wedding, followed a few pages later by passionate letters about what untaxed Internet commerce will do to independent bookstores and to the community such places encourage. San Francisco institutions such as Finocchio's—probably the nation's longest running drag-queen revue—have lost their leases. Fear and eviction come up every day. My favorite example is a letter to "Ask Isadora," the *San Francisco Bay Guardian*'s sex-advice column, by a masochist who wanted to know whether he really had to obey his dominatrix by sexually servicing their ancient landlord. Though the issue for him was about the extent to which submissiveness must go, the issue for her was preserving the lease by any means necessary. San Francisco's housing crisis makes even dominatrixes cower.

"Where will you go?" is the question tenants ask each other, and the answer is always another city, another state. A woman who works at a domestic violence shelter tells me that the entire premise of domestic violence counseling—that the spouse should leave the batterer—is being undermined by the lack of places for such victims to go beyond the temporary shelters. For landlords, housing is an investment, but for tenants it's the terms on which the most intimate aspects of their lives are played out: home. This is a private psychological crisis as well as a public economic one, and just as homelessness can make people outright crazy so the threat of it can strain character.

I drop by Global Exchange, the human rights and environmental organization that did much to rally opposition to the World Trade Organization in Seattle at the end of 1999, and meet its director, Medea Benjamin. She tells me that a dot-com has just rented the space below them on this scruffy stretch of Mission Street, and they're probably facing an unaffordable rent increase. A little further down Mission Street, the Bay View Bank Building, an office building housing clinics, Spanish-language media, and nonprofits, was leased to a dot-com, which is evicting them all. In the old days of gentrification, getting bounced from a neighborhood meant you just landed somewhere else, but in this game of musical chairs, the only available chairs are over the horizon. The day I read that the Pacific Stock Exchange is going to close, I run into Cliff Hengst and find out that he's going to lose his Mission Street home of nine years. The Stock Exchange is closing because the new economy is virtual: it doesn't require locations. Cliff is losing his home because the people who work in the new economy aren't virtual, and they make more money than he does. The apartment he shares with his boyfriend Scott and the auto body shop below it will be torn down to make way for condos. Cliff knows four artists who've moved to L.A. in the last month, he tells me, and he figures he'll move there, too, since no one like him can afford to relocate within the city. I figure San Francisco without Cliff will be just a subtle bit bleaker. Your basic half-Indonesian gay San Francisco artist, Cliff has contributed to the city in countless ways, like a lot of the others who are heading into exile.

In times of tyranny, the citizens talk of democracy and justice; in our time we talk of public space, architecture, housing, urban design, cultural geography, community and landscape—which suggests that the current crises are located in location itself. Geography may be the central discipline of our time, as visual art, literature, film, history all take up questions of place. Car-based suburbia has been a particularly nowheresville version of utopia since the Second World War, but the spread of chains, the gentrification of cities, the ability of administrators to control increasingly subtle details of public space and public life all threaten to make urban places as bland and inert as suburbia, to erase place. Much has been said about the New Urbanism, whereby suburbs are designed to resemble small towns, but what is happening in San Francisco and cities across the country is a new New Urbanism in which cities function like suburbs.

This is a story about love and money. Or a story about love, money and location. The new economy is as different from the old economy as a tourist economy is to the remote village it suddenly lands in; the campesinos can't afford those hotel rooms and drinks, and San Franciscans can't afford the transformed San Francisco. As things we took for granted vanish day by day, San Franciscans' love for their city becomes more and more evident. People speak constantly, obsessively, of what is happening and mourn what is being lost. Several photographers devote themselves to documenting the vanishing places—the same kind of salvage photography once used to document vanishing fourth world cultures and crafts or that Eugene Atget and Charles Marville used to capture a vanishing Paris. The artist Chip Lord makes a video documentary on what the new technology is doing to San Francisco's public spaces and civic life. A few people calling themselves the Mission Yuppie Eradication Project put up posters calling for class war. The Mission Artists Gentrification Insurrection organizes a March of the Evicted, and its posters with a brilliant graphic by Lower East Side artist Eric Drooker linger on the streets long afterwards. People hold meetings, work on eviction defenses, write letters to the editor. Everyone talks about the transformation of the city, and almost every tenant talks about fear of losing his or her perch here. It's in the news every day. It is the main news here, and has been for the last few years. It's a crisis, a boom, and an obsession.

Love of place should not be confused with nationalism, which is a ferocious identification with an abstract idea or an ethnicity. To love one's place is to love particulars, details, routines, memories, minutia, strangers, encounters, surprises. It's common now for lovers of rural places to fight to preserve them, and what they love is usually the appearance of a place, the activities possible in that place, sometimes the fauna as well as the flora and form, but also what that place means. Love of a city is a more complicated thing, in that it's a love of one's fellow humans in quantity, for their eccentricities and frailties, as well as a love of buildings, institutions such as Halloween in the Castro or the Chinese New Year Parade, particular places, ethnic mixes; but also a love of one's own liberation by and in connection to these phenomena. What is happening here eats out the heart of the city from the inside: the infrastructure is for the most part being added to rather than torn down, but the life within it is being drained away, a siphoning off of diversity, cultural life, memory, complexity. What remains will look like the city that was—or like a brighter, shinier, tidier version of it—but what it contained will be gone. It will be a hollow city.

Every day somebody's apartment or house is turned from a home into a commodity and put on the market, and they join the ranks of the displaced. A steady stream of the displaced is trouping to the East Bay, where they are accelerating the gentrification of Oakland and Berkeley, whose poor are in turn moving further from the center themselves. As Paul Rauber put it in an *East Bay Express* article about this ripple effect, "That means Arun boots Deidre, who boots Miguel, who crosses the bay to boot Shawana."[10] But many—the poor as well as artists—are leaving the Bay Area altogether. Susan Miller, executive director of New Langton Arts, estimates that 30 to 40 percent of the artists here a few years ago have left: Film Arts Foundation, for example, is not only losing its lease but its constituency of independent filmmakers. American Indian Contemporary Arts, a downtown nonprofit gallery, was evicted last fall in favor of a dot-com, and probably won't be able to find a replacement location.[11] San Francisco's rich cultural life arises out of a European-style density (it has the densest population in the US outside New York) and out of the combination of many ethnicities, classes, media, resources, seekers after the adventure of making culture, revolution, identity. These things are not portable; you can move the species but not the habitat.

Of course, this is happening is because San Francisco is such a desirable place. The story goes that the first wave of technology workers were just electronics and software geeks who were content to live in the suburban sprawl of Silicon Valley, but along with the Internet came a more hip technocracy demanded nightlife, grit and sensibility. Just as tourists can love a place into unrecognizability and homogeneity, so these young workers and their older bosses and backers may eviscerate the city. Some of them are buying art, and sales are booming for a few artists—but that doesn't counterbalance the impact on the arts community as a whole. Even the *Wall Street Journal* notes that the dot-com newcomers like cover bands more than innovative ones, and so San Francisco's famously creative music scene is withering as well.[12] Whatever the Internet may be bringing the masses stranded far from civilization, the Internet economy in its capital is producing a massive cultural die-off, not a flowering.

San Francisco used to be the great anomaly. What happened here was interesting precisely because it was different from what was happening anywhere else. We were a sanctuary for the queer, the eccentric, the creative, the radical, the political and economic refugees, and so they came and reinforced the city's difference. In some ways the city's difference goes all the way back to the Gold Rush, when the absence of traditional social structures, the overwhelmingly young and male population, and wild fluctuations of wealth produced independent women, orgiastic behavior, epidemics of violence and an atmosphere of liberation. "They had their faults," the San Francisco poet Kenneth Rexroth once remarked of San Francisco's original inhabitants, "but they were not influenced by Cotton

Labor Day parade on Market Street, 1935 (damaged photo). Courtesy San Francisco Public Library.

Mather."[13] For many decades afterwards, the city was celebrated as a cosmopolitan version of the Wild West town, with malleable social mores, eccentrics and adventurers a big part of the social mix. By the twentieth century, it was becoming a center for immigrant Italian anarchists, Wobblies and union organizers— "not only the most tightly organized city in America but ... the stronghold of trade unionism in the United States," asserted Carey McWilliams.[14] Conscientious objectors flocked here after World War II, and the poets who would later be celebrated as beat and as the San Francisco Renaissance started coming in the 1940s and 1950s; African-American emigration to the wartime jobs of San Francisco produced another postwar cultural flourishing of jazz and nightlife. With bars like the Black Cat, it was also a haven for gays and lesbians early on, and remains one today for those who can afford it. It was the place where the counterculture of what gets called "the sixties" flourished most, as well as a major center for punk culture and related subversions after 1977.

Throughout the 1980s, it was a sanctuary city for refugees from the Central American wars, and the movements sometimes called multiculturalism flourished here, from the environmental justice movement to the 1980s explosion of visual arts dealing with questions of ethnicity and identity. And of course since the Sierra Club was founded here in 1892, the San Francisco Bay Area has been a major center for environmental activism and the evolution of environmental ideas. Feminism, human rights activism, pacifism, Buddhism, paganism, alternative medicine, dance, rock and roll, jazz are some of the other phenomena infusing the local culture. The city has also changed radically many times. In 1960, it was 78 percent white, but by 1980 whites were less than 50 percent of the population and it was the nation's most ethnically diverse large city (with a diversity similar in many ways to what it had during the Gold Rush).[15] But San Francisco's is a history of pruning as well as blooming: since the 1950s San Francisco has been mutating from a blue-collar port city of manual labor and material goods to a white-collar center of finance, administration, tourism and, now, the "knowledge industries." Since 1997 this change has accelerated spectacularly. As Randy Shaw, executive director of the Tenderloin Housing Clinic, put it, we have had fifteen years of change compressed into a couple of dozen months, and nobody saw it coming.

This is a story about love, but there is also a lot of anger. Some people have focused on "newcomers," and a sardonic discussion of what constitutes a San Franciscan—how many years, what kind of habits—filled the letters page of the *SF Weekly* for a while. Some people have focused on yuppies, and there is definitely tension on both sides of that divide—those who know they are considered yuppies, and those who hate whoever qualifies as a yuppie in their eyes. Some people have said that it's not the fault of those who came here looking for a job that there's a housing crisis, and it's the local politicos, real estate speculators, greedy landlords and developers who should be targeted. Some fault a system in which a basic human need—housing—exists largely as a free-market commodity, so that need takes a back seat to profit.

My own writing has been about culture and politics in other senses. I have written about senses of place, and the geography of culture, about specific issues and sites, as well as about particular artists and movements. Lately it seems to me that even to be able to recognize and resist the forces that threaten the environments and communities that sustain us requires time and space that are rapidly eroding: time eroding as an ever-more-expensive world presses us to produce and consume ever more rapidly, catapults information and distraction at us, eliminates the unstructured time for musing and meeting; space eroding as public space, access to the sites of power, culture and protest—and also the unexploited space where one can hear one's own thoughts—is undermined. My last book was a history of walking, and it is in part an exploration of the circumstances in which culture, contemplation and community are possible and of the embodied and geographically grounded basis of thinking and imagining. This book is about a more gritty version of the same subject: San Francisco has been not only the great refuge for the nation's pariahs and non-conformists; it has been the breeding ground of new ideas, mores and movements social, political and artistic. To see the space in which those things were incubated be homogenized into just another place for over-paid-but-overworked producer-consumers is to witness a great loss, not only for the experimentalists, but for the world that has benefited from the better experiments (and been entertained by the sillier ones). Think of San Francisco as both a laboratory of the new and a preserve for the old subversive functionality of cities. Think about what happens if both these aspects get bulldozed by the technology economy. The Internet too may be a laboratory for the new, but even if it is a great organizing tool it is not presently of much value for social critique or the expression of cultural genius.

A 1971 documentary about San Francisco titled "The City That Waits to Die" presumed that San Francisco would be destroyed by its unstable geology, but the earthquake that has come at the millennium has been a temblor of capital and its unstable distribution, altering San Francisco more than could almost any natural disaster. This book is not about the new technology economy, nor is it an economic history of cities or gentrification. It is a portrait of what a sudden economic boom is doing to a single city and a reflection on what is being lost and what its value—its nonmonetary value—is. It focuses almost entirely on San Francisco, not because what is happening here is unique, but because it so resembles what is happening elsewhere that I believe it can stand alone as an example of a crisis in American cities. *Hollow City* focuses on artists, particularly visual artists, because artists are the indicator species of this ecosystem: from their situation can be gauged the overall breadth or shrinkage of the margin for noncommercial activity, whether that activity is artistic, political, spiritual or social.

A few days after my excursion to the Coltrane church and the park, I go to see Chris Carlsson in his office on Market Street, a big room that with its posters, clippings, abandoned coffee cups, bicycles and beat-up furniture looks more like the living room of an activist household than anyplace else I visit now—and it is an activist household of sorts, both the site for Chris's typesetting business and a gathering place for myriad political activities. In 1981 Chris cofounded *Processed World,* a situationist magazine analyzing and promoting subversion of the white-collar workplace. Along with Re/Search publications and the punk-and-populist-politics magazine *Maximum Rock'n'Roll, P.W.* represents a little-recognized punk-culture golden age for alternative publishing (*Processed World* folded in 1993, but the other two grind on). In the mid-1990s Chris cofounded Critical Mass, the collective bicycle ride that has since become a global phenomenon to protest the lack of safe space for bicycle transit and to create that space. For a few days in 1997, San Francisco's Critical Mass became a national news story about bicyclists' confrontation with the law and with Mayor Willie Brown. Chris's concerns with public space, technology and social life continued with the City Lights anthology *Reclaiming San Francisco* he co-edited, and with his CD-ROM *Shaping San Francisco* expanding on that history installed in two independent bookstores and the main library to prove that the new technologies need not be privatizing. A guy whose hectic conversational pace seems younger than his forty-something years and whose nearly white, sea-captainish beard seems older, he settled down on one of the thrashed couches in front of a bookcase full of San Francisco's history to give me his version.

"I've lived here since 1978. I came here as a twenty-one-year-old guy and got a job with an environmental group doing canvassing and thought, This is it, I want to live in San Francisco. At that point Haight Street was fifty percent boarded up and overrun with alcohol and heroin and there was no sense of gentrification being around the corner at all. When I got here it felt kind of bleak and slumlike. I didn't know what to expect and didn't have a sense of the previous cultures. The punk scene was unfolding around me, and the city's been reshaping itself around me ever since. I have a sense of connectedness to San Francisco as this site of change. There's something very exciting about the endless influx of new energy looking for something inexplicably magical. Everybody keeps coming here to renew that quest or had until now. And that's exactly what I think we're losing at this moment, this endless arrival of the young, the radical, the political and the marginal and the edgy. They're not coming here anymore. If they do come here, they can't stay or they've gotta find themselves a six-day-a-week job, which is what people here think is an acceptable mode.

"It's ironic that, in a city that was the founding place of the eight-hour day in the 1860s, there's no eight-hour day anymore 140 years later. This is the first city in North America where the eight-hour day was really established. The first technological coup against organized labor was the transcontinental railroad, which broke the back of the eight-hour day in San Francisco. The railroad builders brought all the unemployed laborers back from the east, but before the railroad was finished there was a tight labor market. The workers who were here at the end of the Civil War realized, 'Hey, we can control this,' and so they published decrees in the local newspapers announcing the eight-hour day. Group after group did that, and in 1867 they had a march of a thousand workers up Market Street marching in the order by which their trade had established the eight-hour day—but by '72 it was gone.

The St. John Coltrane congregation arrives at its temporary home.

"Now we live in a world in which the eight-hour day is not only a wistful memory for a lot of people, but they don't even conceptualize it as an issue. You individually have to deal with remaining competitive in the market, and the number of hours you work is just not a relevant issue to band together with other people about, because there's no sense of class, no sense of shared commitment. You are an independent entrepreneur in the world. Your job is to work as much and as long as you can in the labor market. It's a laughable predicament, and there's not much time to find your way out of it, it's a bit of a rat's maze. And that's speedup. That's my experience of San Francisco: we are living through the greatest speedup in human history, and nobody's even saying it out loud."

"Is there a dot-com culture?"

"No, there's no culture, we're all greedy . . . no, that's a joke. A few months ago in *Fortune* magazine there was an article called "The Dot-com Way." The priority is definitely making money—fast. It's a multicultural business—or maybe forced to be. It's hard to find skilled people, so you're drawing from everywhere in the world: Asia, Africa, India, Europe—anywhere skills have been acquired.

"It's a fast-paced industry, with long hours and constant learning—though sometimes it's not the money, it's the adrenaline."

Tools for Managing Loyalty

"The company is in e-marketing. We provide
loyalty solutions. We build the technology that
makes people come back to a website.
We think of it as a tool that manages loyalty
between customer and company.

"Most of the people in this business
are very young, and they don't all have
experience in communication.
So you have to reconcile that with
this space we work in. There are lots
of places to sit and meet: couches,
outdoor tables, the pool table.
It's a casual environment."

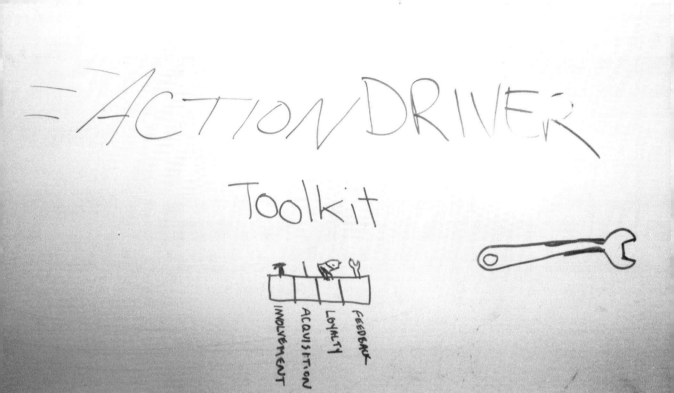

=ACTION DRIVER

Toolkit

FEEDBACK
LOYALTY
ACQUISITION
INVOLVEMENT

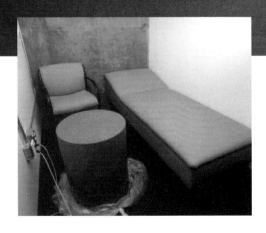

"This company was founded in the late '90s. When I came on board there were 80 people. We now have over 400 employees, including all the acquisitions we've made.

"Now that the company is so large, it's hard to know what's going on. We talk a lot about how to make people happy. How do we make displaced people happy in a new company?"

I feel bad that the dot-com movement is the first trend in this city that's pushing people out. It's all about economics. I'm in this industry and I think it should be more socially responsible. We're becoming this technological, scientific center. I think science can hurt social life. – *Financial Systems Analyst*

Vacant lot, Western Addition, 1950s. Photograph by David Johnson.

Vacant lot, Western Addition, 2000.

The Shopping Cart and the Lexus

Campaigns to get rid of the poor have a long history in San Francisco. African Americans, working-class seniors, other residential-hotel denizens and the homeless have all had their turn, and other campaigns—against undocumented immigrants and refugees and against Latinos and Asians generally—have attempted to erase or undermine populations on a larger scale. As the Second World War was ending, the city came up with a master plan that featured elements of redevelopment, and by the beginning of 1947 specific proposals were being made to annihilate portions of the Western Addition. *Blight* was the magical word of the era of urban renewal, a word whose invocation justified the destruction of housing, communities and neighborhoods in many American cities, and San Francisco was no exception. The Western Addition had, not coincidentally, become home to San Francisco's African-American community, and urban renewal would eventually be nicknamed "Negro removal." Earlier in the century, according to the African-American historian Albert S. Broussard, African Americans had lived in various parts of the city, but as large num-

43

bers of southern Blacks arrived to participate in the wartime economy a backlash of discrimination and segregation had reconcentrated the Black community (between 1940 and 1950, the Black population increased ninefold, to 43,460). Broussard writes, "Blacks occupied a disproportionate share of the Western Addition's substandard housing relative to their percentage of the city's population. Overcrowding, unsanitary living quarters, and infestations of rodents were typical sights, particularly in the city's Fillmore district."[1]

The Western Addition's eastern edge had been home to a Jewish immigrant population, and its northern side had been Japanese until the internment camps were opened in early 1942. Kenneth Rexroth was among the artists and radicals who organized to protect Japanese Americans from internment; he and his wife, Marie Kass Rexroth, hid several young people in their Potrero Hill home, and the Fellowship of Reconciliation organized a program that allowed many to go east to school rather than into the bleak internment camps (at Rexroth's prompting, the Fellowship had already founded the American Committee to Protect the Civil Rights of Americans of Oriental Ancestry).[2] Maya Angelou was one of the southerners who came to the Western Addition as a child, and she writes in *I Know Why the Caged Bird Sings*, "In the early months of World War II, San Francisco's Fillmore district, or the Western Addition, experienced a visible revolution.... The Yakamoto Sea Food Market quietly became Sammy's Shoe Shine Parlor and Smoke Shop. Yashigira's Hardware metamorphosed into La Salon de Beaute owned by Miss Clorinda Jackson. The Japanese shops which sold products to Nisei customers were taken over by enterprising Negro businessmen, and in less than a year became permanent homes away from home for the newly arrived Southern Blacks. Where the odor of tempura, raw fish and cha had dominated, the aroma of chitlings, greens and ham hocks now prevailed. The Asian population dwindled before my eyes.... No member of my family and none of the family friends ever mentioned the absent Japanese. It was as if they had never owned or lived in the houses we inhabited."[3]

The housing conditions were sometimes vile, but they were the result rather than the cause of social problems (the poet Michael McClure, who visited many of the homes while working for the census in 1960, remembers them as airy and gracious).[4] Nevertheless, urban renewal went forward, propelled by the peculiar official belief that problems caused by poverty and racism could be cured by architecture—often architecture that would exclude the removed population (just as homelessness is now often addressed by attempting to make the homeless go away—not into houses, just out of sight or out of town).

Victorian houses that were removed in the 1950s. "They were on the property where the Fillmore Center was going to be—so they were in the way. Theoretically, everyone who lived there got vouchers, so they could be the first to move back in." Photograph by David Johnson, 1949.

By the time urban renewal in the Western Addition had begun its second campaign, the San Francisco Redevelopment Agency could write, "San Francisco is now developing programs to correct blighted and congested conditions and to deal with an accumulation of housing that is continuously aging and deteriorating faster than it is being rehabilitated or replaced. The study area contains an estimated 1008 residential structures, many of which are in various degrees of deterioration and in need of rebuilding or replacement. More than 50 percent of the structures are past middle age with an estimated average age of sixty-seven years. It is this condition which results in neighborhood blight and calls for both major public improvement and private rehabilitation and reconstruction."[5] The

Jazz Club, Hunters Point, 1956. Photograph by David Johnson.

Western Addition's building stock consisted largely of Victorian houses, the highly ornate wooden "painted ladies" San Francisco is famous for, and some of the best examples still stand in areas that escaped redevelopment. Today, many of them sell for a million dollars apiece: that they are for the most part structurally sound half a century after redevelopment began suggests how gratuitous were its official premises. The report went on to condemn the neighborhood because single-family houses had been converted into apartments, convalescent hospitals and rooming houses and because "stores, industry and houses are haphazardly intermingled." (It is just this intermingling that suburban design sought to eliminate and that Jane Jacobs's 1961 manifesto, *The Death and Life of Great American Cities*, celebrates as key to the vitality of urban life.)

None of the reports mentions that Fillmore Street had become the Harlem of the West, where jazz clubs and a lively nightlife flourished. My octogenarian neighbor who emigrated to the Western Addition from Texas around the time of the Second World War still speaks fondly of the elegant arches of lights that used to adorn Fillmore Street, of the six movie theaters, the many hotels with wonderful jazz clubs, the liveliness of the street at all hours. "It was such a nice place to go," he says, shaking his head. After urban renewal, the Fillmore was never the same, and for decades its central expanse consisted of vacant lots surrounded by cyclone fences (in the 1980s, high-rise residences were finally built on the lots from which the Fillmore's heart had been extracted). As resistance to urban renewal grew, the justifications for carrying it out grew more hysterical. In a vicious document dated July 1964, the Redevelopment Agency wrote of "blight consolidated and seemingly permanent in the area, accompanied by its environmental associate, social degradation."[6] The area was condemned for its high proportion of tenants to owners and for lenders' reluctance to invest in the area, as well as for higher than average levels of transience, single-parent house-holds, unemployment and juvenile delin-quency. One chart demonstrated that venereal disease, tuberculosis, and infant deaths were higher in the area; no chart reported what Broussard does, that "although many black doctors had migrated to San Francisco during World War II, only one black physician for every 6,667 black residents practiced in San Francisco, in sharp contrast with the city-wide ratio of one doctor per 475 residents."[7] The city's redevelopment mani-festoes seem at least implicitly a counter-argument to the Civil Rights Movement;

Fillmore Street, 1950s. Photograph by David Johnson.

they argue a different set of causes than racism, exclusion and poverty for the condition of nonwhite inner-city inhabitants, and a different cure than social justice—or argue that modernist architecture is social justice, a shaky premise even then.

Of course the real motives for redevelopment had nothing to do with reform. As one standard American history puts it, "Mayors, bankers, and real estate interests found federal funding of urban renewal planning far more profitable than expenditures on low-income families. Central city slums fell before the onslaught of federally funded bulldozers. Gleaming office towers, civic centers, and apartment projects for middle- and upper-income citizens replaced the slums."[8] In the postwar era, San Francisco's business leaders saw an opportunity to position the city as capital of the Pacific Rim. It may have been inevitable that white-collar admin-istrative jobs would largely replace blue-collar port and manufacturing

More Than Half-Way Home
As most San Franciscans know, the Western Addition is blessed with some of the City's best weather.
It is also within walking distance of the Civic Center and just a quick bus ride from Downtown.
And now its renewal (Western Addition Redevelopment Areas A-1 and A-2) is more than 50 per cent complete.
Just look around—

Redevelopment Agency brochure, 1971.

jobs, but there were numerous ways in which this transformation could have unfolded. For the most part, however, the transformation has been marked not only be disregard for the city's poor and working class but by outright hostility to them. The business leaders of the 1950s and 1960s looked around for sites in which this scenario could be imposed most aggressively. One area was the Golden Gateway, San Francisco's Les Halles: the food market and a few hundred residents were evicted for what eventually became the high-rise-and-plaza Embarcadero Center complex near the foot of Market Street (where on Saturdays an upscale farmers' market reiterates in miniature what was lost).

The first stage of urban renewal in the Western Addition had similar results: the area around Geary Boulevard and Fillmore Street was razed, and in place of the Victorian houses came cement modernism. As the San Francisco architect Eric Fang writes, "Following modernist doctrine, Demars' plan populated these superblocks with high-rise residential towers set within landscaped plazas. Unfortunately, to accommodate parking requirements, these plazas were set atop parking garages called podiums. These projects, designed by Stone Marraccini and Patterson and Daniel Mann Johnson and Mendenhall and completed in the mid- to late-60s, not only introduced a new scale to this part of the city but demonstrated the deadening effect this type of urbanism could have on the streets and spaces in between the buildings."[9] Ironically, a mall-like version of Japantown was rebuilt, backed by investors from Japan and opposed by

Langston Hughes at a party in the Western Addition, 1949.
Photograph by David Johnson.

many in the local Japanese-American community (which had dispersed after returning from the internment camps following World War II). Elsewhere in the Western Addition, bauhaus bunkers were built to house some of the African Americans displaced by urban renewal, but a significant portion of the 4,000 families evicted were unable to move back at all, and the second phase of urban renewal displaced another 13,500 residents of the Western Addition. Chester Hartman, who has written extensively about urban renewal in San Francisco, concludes that the Redevelopment Agency "became a powerful and aggressive army out to capture as much downtown land as it could.... The Agency turned to systematically sweeping out the poor, with the full backing of the city's power elite."[10]

In the Western Addition, urban renewal met with a mixed response: some believed the promises, some opposed them, and many leaders sought to make them more palatable or to advance their own agendas. In Hunters Point, a neighborhood that had grown up around the wartime shipyards on the city's southeast waterfront, redevelopment brought genuine improvements to the African Americans who remained its majority population. And in the South of Market area, what may have been the fiercest war in all of American redevelopment was fought. South of Market had a brief tenure in the 1860s as a gracious district for the moderately wealthy, but it has been a working-class and immigrant district ever since. By the postwar era, its numerous residential hotels housed a predominantly male and elderly population, particularly in the area known as Yerba Buena, just across Market Street from downtown's prime business and shopping district. Though blight was cited as grounds for razing the area, it was clear that expansion of commercial and civic functions was the real motive. The hotelier and real estate mogul Ben Swig had been the first to propose redevelopment in 1954, and he donated money to the Redevel-

The Mercantile Building, with what would become Yerba Buena Center in the background. Sandblasting has since removed all vestiges of the past from its sides. Photograph by Janet Delaney, 1980.

opment Agency to prepare a study. Commenting that the study was meant to "find the most expeditious way of declaring the area of Mr. Swig's interest a blighted area," Joseph Alioto, the agency's new director and the city's future mayor, returned the money.[11] Nevertheless, the plans went forward, and in 1969 many of those who would be affected formed Tenants and Owners in Opposition to Redevelopment (TOOR) and went to court.

The population was overwhelmingly white, male, retired and union. Many had been maritime workers, and most hailed from the heyday of unions, strikes and organizing, from San Francisco's General Strike of 1934 and other moments when labor had contested for power. Some had been communists. They prized the security, affordability, community and access the area's forty-eight residential hotels provided, and they were not going to be herded out of their homes like sheep. As Calvin Welch, an affordable housing activist in the city since 1970, recalls, "A very sharp battle was fought, much more sharp than the Western Addition. People were killed, buildings were burnt. Political organizations were suppressed. It was much more hostile. Unfortunately what that produced was the loss of an opportunity to create a common front against urban renewal. The agency became masters at planting racial and class tensions to ensure that there was no effective coalition. There were two attempts to create a common organization for the people of the Western Addition [and] the people South of Market to take on redevelopment. There were great tragedies. One of the tragedies was that the failure stemmed from the racism of the South of Market men. They

From inside out: view of Yerba Buena Gardens from Sony Metreon, 2000.

were overwhelmingly white and overwhelmingly racist. They saw African Americans as sellouts. They were so opposed to any compromise [that] they probably cut the best deal that was ever cut with urban renewal in the city."[12] Though they ended up with a net loss of rooms, the TOOR activists delayed hotel destruction and forced the city to provide better relocation support and to build a few large residential facilities for seniors.

Still, South of Market was gutted to make way for Yerba Buena Center. The convention center, named after assassinated Mayor George Moscone, opened in December 1981. For several years the space in front of Moscone Center remained a vacant lot. When the Democratic Convention was held there in 1984, the gravelly dirt became a "free speech zone" where local punk bands such as MDC (Multi-Death Corporations) played and thousands met to protest the business-as-usual Democrats with marches, blockades, "die-ins," and Hall of Shame tours of downtown's many corporate headquarters, such as Bechtel, Chevron and Bank of America.[13] Hundreds were jailed and several were injured in one melee when San

Francisco mounted police intentionally trampled activists. Now a complex featuring a theater, a Martin Luther King commemorative fountain of big concrete slabs, and a center for showcasing local art, the place has a strangely dislocated, airportlike ambience, though its central lawn provides a pleasant lunch spot for office workers and an occasional site for performances, concerts and outdoor sculpture shows. The place has a perpetual identity crisis about whether it belongs to the high-minded nonprofit sector or to the tourism-and-entertainment industry that the area as a whole clearly caters to. Across from the Center for the Arts is the most recent addition to Yerba Buena Center: the glittering silver-and-glass Sony Metreon, billed as "an interactive entertainment experience." It harbors a multiplex movie theater for Hollywood movies, a few knick-knack stores, including a Discovery Channel boutique, a Starbucks coffeeshop, a Sony PlayStation for electronic games, and the world's first Microsoft Store. A more obsequious monument to global capitalism would be hard to find.

According to its website, the place is now dedicated to "serving San Francisco's diverse communities," and it's a complicated argument whether democracy and culture are better served by a collection of residential hotels occupied by old white radicals, a vacant lot occupied by mostly white political punks, or by a private–public complex for sometimes-multicultural arts and entertainment (even the visual art center has lent itself to some very commercial enterprises such as *The Art of Star Wars*, though it also regularly shows the young and emerging artists of San Francisco). Chelsea Piers in Manhattan had a similar evolution, from maritime workplace to derelict ruins cruised by gay outlaws like David Wojnarowicz to its current highly managed exercise and recreation facilities—from a place for labor and laborers to a place for leisure consumption with a temporary autonomous zone of subversion in between. Probably the best melding of these histories ever was Ira Nowinski's 1995 Center for the Arts show of his early 1970s photographs of the TOOR activists, their homes, and their demonstrations. In beautiful black-and-white images, Nowinski suggested a minimal lifestyle that was more than acceptable for many who came out of both the working class and the Depression. His still lifes of folded linens and pillows atop sagging striped mattresses, hotel lobby signs, and then the closed and wrecked hotels radiated a potent melancholy. To see these still lifes and sympathetic portraits in Yerba Buena Center for the Arts was to see a place get its ghosts back: standing in front of the images one could imagine that one stood where a wall had been or an old man had laid down to dream, an erased architecture that still exercised authority over the shiny new spaces. More recently, Nowinski's photographs have been shown a few blocks southeast, in a gallery in South Park, the gracious old oval of Victorians now famous as the center of Multimedia Gulch. (Before the Internet, South Park had harbored a thriving Filipino community.) There too Nowinski's images exercise a fascinating pull as reminders to the young technocrats of when the region belonged to the old, to the poor and to manual laborers. These photographs testify to something else, too: the many roles artists can play in cities and conflicts. Among the other artists documenting the Yerba Buena conflict in the 1970s are Connie Hatch and Janet Delaney. (Along the same lines, the photographer Lewis Watts saved the photo collection from Red Powell's Shine Parlor on Fillmore Street, a marvelous array of publicity shots of the musicians who came through in the 1940s and 1950s, restored them, and reinstalled them in the nearby New Chicago Barbershop.)

In the late 1950s San Franciscans fought to prevent the freeway system from completely garroting the city and ripping through Golden Gate Park to the Pacific Ocean (and the 1989 earthquake gave its support to this cause by shattering the Embarcadero Freeway and parts of the Central

Freeway, which have since been cleared away). More genteel individuals and groups did much to save the cable cars and protect Victorian houses and historic neighborhoods. But after Yerba Buena, a younger group of radicals began to take on housing issues. When the hundred-room International Hotel was threatened with destruction, many groups came out in force. Located where North Beach, Chinatown and the Financial District meet, the I-Hotel housed Filipino and Chinese elders with nowhere to go. This time the displacement was carried out by private enterprise—real estate tycoon Walter Shorenstein sold the building to a Hong Kong corporation when his plan to turn it into a parking garage was squelched, and the Hong Kong corporation proceeded with the evictions. Among those organizing the resistance was Emile de Guzman, who had grown up around César Chávez's United Farmworkers, and support of various kinds came from the Weathermen and Jim Jones's Peoples Temple (whose home base in the Western Addition provided an outlet, however problematic, for those traumatized by urban renewal before many of them died in Guyana). A crowd of five thousand met the four hundred policemen and sheriff's deputies who finally evicted the last remaining residents in 1977. The building was emptied and demolished; today it remains a gaping hole with only graffiti along with Curtis Choy's documentary film, *The Fall of the I-Hotel,* to preserve its memory today.[14]

Lewis Watts holds a photograph he salvaged and installed in Reggie Pettus's New Chicago Barbershop #3.

By the mid-1970s activists and progressive publications were organizing against the "Manhattanization" of San Francisco, by which they meant

View of redeveloped Fillmore
Street from New Chicago Barbershop #3.

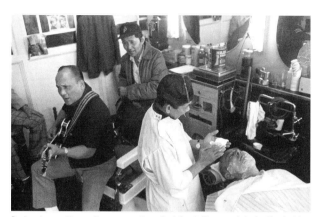

Barbershop on Kearny Street across from the I-Hotel. Photograph by Ira Nowinski.

Demonstration at the I-Hotel just before the evictions. Photograph by Ira Nowinski.

the development of high-rises downtown with the concomitant influx of white-collar workers seeking housing in the city. As professionals and managers began to discover the pleasures of urban life (and the horrors of commuting), housing prices began to escalate. In the early 1980s, tenant activists managed to win passage of citywide residential rent control. Though it has significant problems, notably the lack of vacancy control, rent control has done much to preserve affordable housing for those who arrived and stayed before the current rental-rate explosion. (Rent control is why I can afford to write this book.) Other activists came together in the early 1980s to protect the residential hotels of the Tenderloin from being destroyed or converted into tourist hotels; attorney-activist Randy Shaw, who was one of the principals in that battle, declares from his desk at the Tenderloin Housing Clinic that this housing stock is permanently protected. Yet another significant victory was Proposition M in 1986, which put a number of limits on downtown growth, required office buildings to ameliorate their impact with contributions to transit, low-cost housing and other necessities for the city, and made it policy to pro-

tect industrial districts, neighborhood businesses, neighborhood
character, historic buildings and
other elements of a diversified,
civilized city. Rent control and
Proposition M represent an era
when activists took the initiative
to set housing and development
policy, rather than just fighting
rearguard actions against market
forces and policies set by others.

The poor continued to arrive,
as well as to be driven out. But
the economic situation had permanently changed. Wages began

Chief counsel Tony Kline discussing the
terms of settlement with the membership at
a TOOR meeting, Milner Hotel, 1973. Photograph by Ira Nowinski.

to stagnate in the 1970s, and in the 1980s Reaganism stripped away
resources and services for those at the bottom. Hundreds of thousands of
residential hotel rooms disappeared, and the space in which to be civilly
poor itself began to shrink. What had once been a small population of
outcasts began to become the huge armies of homeless who still haunt
America's streets today. Activists were no longer fighting to defend the
poor but themselves as social darwinism spread to affect the middle
class. As Anders Corr writes in *No Trespassing: Squatting, Rent Strikes, and
Land Struggles Worldwide*, "As a result of soaring rents, small-business failures, and massive corporate layoffs, landlords evicted thousands onto
the streets. These new homeless, who were sometimes well-educated,
drug- and alcohol-free, mentally stable, and, until recently, middle-class,
joined the traditional homeless who more often suffered from addiction
or mental problems. While the new homeless were more likely to get

International Hotel, 1977. Photograph by Ira Nowinski.

off the street quickly, their proximity to homelessness (just one paycheck away, they reminded themselves) encouraged them to lend support to the homeless left behind. In addition to traditional homeless advocacy, hundreds of homeless organizations that used squatting as a tactic sprouted across the nation."[15] Officially, homelessness was treated much like "blight": rather than attempting to address the root causes, city elites and administrators attempted to hide the human results, whether it meant tearing down housing or criminalizing homelessness and driving the unhoused from place to place or into vile "shelters."

Since the 1980s, the *Chronicle* has been publishing letters to the editor by writers who claim their outings to the park or the opera have been ruined by the sight of the destitute; their point is not that the homeless pose ethical and economic challenges to the housed, but that they are unaesthetic. Most of San Francisco's mayors since the 1980s have responded with punitive measures focusing on clearing certain areas, as well as subsidiary tactics like arresting Food Not Bombs members for serving food to the homeless. Willie Brown, who once proposed using heat-detecting helicopters to rout sleepers from Golden Gate Park, has presided over the elimination of benches from the plaza in front of City Hall and the long-term cyclone-fencing-off of one hangout zone at the head of Haight Street in Golden Gate Park. Corr documents (in a book written in a decades-old collective household in the Western Addition) how from the mid-1990s on Homes Not Jails used squatting aligned with community organizing, public activism and other tactics to try to house the homeless, and how they often—albeit temporarily—succeeded (activists in other communities, notably Seattle, have achieved more permanent victories). Since Homes Not Jails disbanded a year or so ago, several other organizations have sprung up to deal with the burgeoning eviction and homelessness problems. And the new battlefront is the Mission.

The Mission, which survived urban renewal untouched, is facing another force entirely. Gentrification is a cumulative public effect of numerous private, individual acts and thereby far harder to resist than the institutional action of urban renewal. The word itself was first used in 1964 by the British sociologist Ruth Glass, who wrote, "One by one, many of the working-class quarters of London have been invaded by the middle classes—upper and lower.... Once this process of 'gentrification' starts in a district,

Vacant room, Milner Hotel, 1974. Photograph by Ira Nowinski.

it goes on rapidly until all or most of the original working-class occupiers are displaced and the whole social character of the district is changed."[16] In his 1988 book *Neighborhoods in Transition: The Making of San Francisco's Ethnic and Nonconformist Communities*, Brian Godfrey outlines the usual metamorphosis: "In the first stage, a bohemian fringe discovers a neighborhood's special charms—e.g., social diversity, subcultural identification, architectural heritage. Nontraditional 'footloose' elements are favored, such as single people, counter-culturals, homosexuals, artists, feminist households, or college students. These 'urban pioneers' make a run-down or even dangerous area livable and attractive to others who would not normally venture there; they constitute the unintentional 'shock troops' for gentrification and encourage the beginnings of housing speculation. These social elements are not necessarily wealthy in objective terms, but they do often enjoy a conditional affluence, at least insofar as they have more disposable income to spend on renovation because of smaller households and fewer traditional pursuits."[17]

The Castro was one notable neighborhood that was gentrified early on, changing from a mostly elderly, working-class Irish population to a younger gay male population. As Randy Shilts writes in *The Mayor of Castro Street*, his biography of Harvey Milk, "The stolid Irish families sold their Victorians at dirt-cheap prices, fearing greater loss if they waited. By 1973, the numbers of old-timers called the new men of Castro Street—invaders.... At least half of the people moving in were gay, while more and more of the old-timers sold out."[18] According to Godfrey, "Regardless of local fears, property values actually increased by about five times between 1973 and 1976. Police conservatively estimated in 1976 that about 80 gay men a week were moving into San Francisco. By this point, the gay counter-culture had been replaced by a more middle-class, specifically gay community on Castro Street."[19] The affluence of the most visible gay population in San Francisco calls into question the definitions of alternative and subculture; though many gay men here have been social theorists and political activists, the many shops and restaurants of Castro Street gave it the nickname "Cashflow." Recently a huge conflict arose over situating a shelter for homeless queer youth in the Castro; it ended up over the hill in the mostly straight Noe Valley, which objected to less avail.

More commonly the first influx is a sort of pre-gentrification; it consists of people who have more economic mobility, though not necessarily more income, than the earlier residents and who value the existing character of their new neighborhood. Some become community activists. Intolerance seems to arrive with affluence, and the worst thing that can be said about those in the first wave is that they attract the second, affluent influx or at least—especially if they're white—make the neighborhood more palatable and noticeable to those with bigger pocketbooks. By conflating the first influx with the second or holding the first responsible for the second, many analysts of gentrification blame it on artists, and this argument has become a commonplace. For decades, poor white kids—college students, musicians, artists, writers—have been moving into the Mission, which some poor whites never left, but many of the artists and radicals who were raised there or arrived as adults are Latinos (blaming gentrification on artists often presumes that all artists are white). There was a lag of decades—too long for cause-effect principles to prevail—between the first influx and the second. Of course, many of the most hard-working artists have no time for cafés and nightclubs; it's art as a lifestyle rather than a discipline that contributes to changing neighborhoods. On Valencia Street, more and more bookstores and cafés appeared among the bakeries, thrift and hardware stores. Then, in the early 1990s, upscale restaurants began to appear among the cafés and taquerias, followed by clothing and housewares boutiques. The central stretch of Valencia Street has become an upscale restaurant row. More than 50 percent of the businesses there in 1990 had vanished by 1998—and neighborhood commercial rents jumped 42 percent from 1997 to 1999.[20]

For many years, Valencia Street belonged largely to the bohemians and the wealthier who came in their wake, while Mission Street retained the earlier ethnic and economic mix. It was the most literal example of parallel universes, these parallel streets a block apart with their different atmospheres, patrons and kinds of business. In the past few years, however, a few fancy restaurants and bars have come to Mission Street. The artist René Yanez told me that what is now the much-reviled Beauty Bar on Mission Street was once a seedy joint where crack was dealt. Sometimes the problems associated with poverty are eradicated or relocated by gentrification, but that is not a justification for the problems caused by the influx of wealth. As Neil Smith writes in his study of gentrification, "The language of revitalization, recycling, upgrading and renaissance suggests that affected neighborhoods were somehow devitalized or culturally moribund prior to gentrification. While this is sometimes the case, it is often also true that very vital working-class communities are culturally devitalized through gentrification as the new middle class scorns the streets in favor of the dining room and bedroom. The idea of 'urban pioneers' is as insulting applied to contemporary cities as the original idea of 'pioneers' in the US West. Now, as then, it implies that no one lives in the area being pioneered—no one worthy of notice at least."[21] In fact, the Mission has been the center of a vibrant Latino cultural and political community that is being erased by gentrification. But the history of gentrification is tied up with the history of bohemia, and that is another story, or chapter.

John Leanos, Monica Praba Pilar, René García, Gerardo Perez, Jaime Cortez, "Ese—Last of His Tribe" billboard, Galería de la Raza, Mission District, September 2000. The piece is part of the decades-old billboard mural program of the Galería. The text reads in part: "The last known Mexican in the Mission District was captured last night in Delores Park. 'Ese,' the last of his tribe, led a feral Mexican lifestyle in Delores Park, living among the bushes on roots and berries, focaccia crumbs, and leftover bits of antipasti.... Ese formerly shared a small studio with two other young men of the Latino sort but they were unhoused when their space was reclassified from an apartment to an e-partment, with a corresponding rent increase. Ese was shocked to learn that he was the last Mexican in the Mission. When informed that the dishwashers and laborers he saw from the park were all bused in from outside the Digital Zone, he fell silent. Ese is currently under observation at the UC Department of Cultural Anthropology...." Courtesy Galería de la Raza and the artists.

Three Photographers and the Transformation of Yerba Buena

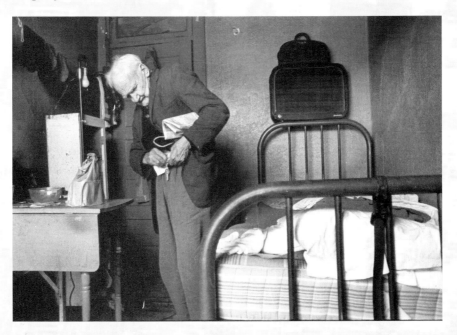

Excerpts from *No Vacancy,* a project by Ira Nowinski

Ira Nowinski:
"In 1970 I read in the newspaper about a hotel that was being torn down to build a Shell station. I went there and I met this guy in front of the building. It was all boarded up and he was moving out. He invited me in. I went upstairs and I photographed him in his room. He had just been in the hospital because he'd been mugged in the alley. He had 4 cents in his pocket. Then his son came and took him away.

"The next day I came back and there were a lot of people and KQED cameras in front of the hotel. It was an action against evicting these people. For the next four years I photographed the process."

Ken Roth in the Rock Hotel, 1971

"The hotels were 'mom and pop' hotels that took care of these old guys. When the Redevelopment Agency took them over they got real shabby. The men literally had to beg for things, like toilet paper. There was a lot of intimidation, like mattresses getting set on fire."

"When I started photographing I didn't know much about hotel life. The rooms were so still and quiet; some had residents and some were empty. In the early 1970s social security was only $120 a month and there were no services for poor single men. Although a lot of them came from big families, they were sort of loners, and some had drinking and emotional problems. But they were also regular guys—very human and considerate of one another."

Joyce Hotel, 1970

Rex Hotel, 1973

"In 1974 after the settlement they each got $5,000, and they disappeared. Some went to Stockton or Sacramento; they were from all different parts of California. Only a few of them actually moved into the new hotels. Mendelsohn House, which was named after Pete, opened just after he died."

"I looked carefully at the photographs the Redevelopment Agency made of this area. After they took over a hotel or shop, they would set up short-term leases and then rent to dirty book stores, or sex novelty shops. They used the photographs of the conditions they created to label this a blighted area so they could demolish it.

"It was a policy to change private space into public space. How do you do it? They had to fabricate a story to make it happen.

"In the nineties when I began to re-work this project—I wanted it to be a part of San Francisco history, so that it isn't just about the Swigs and the Aliotos—to bring the story of these guys into our history."

Photograph by Ira Nowinski, aerial photo and video still, S.F. Redevelopment Agency

Excerpts from FORM FOLLOWS FINANCE, 1979–82
a project by Janet Delaney and Connie Hatch

Corner of Fourth and Folsom:
Demolition of a school, 1980.

Janet Delaney:
"In 1978 I rented a two-bedroom apartment on Langton Street between Folsom and Howard. Most of Yerba Buena had been torn down. I photographed some of the last residences and neighborhood buildings being destroyed."

"At the time I was photographing construction sites. I was in the pit where the Moscone convention center would be built and I realized that this pit was going to be transformed into a building which would impact the entire area. I was really concerned for my neighbors, many of whom had lived in the surrounding neighborhood for years—some their whole lives."

South of Market, 1980; originals in color

A-1 AUTO BODY

We're changing.

DONS MUFFLER

ALL IMPORTS REPAIRED

BRA

WESCO SALES

THIS IS A-1

AUTO BODY SHOP

Pat serving coffee, Budget Hotel, 1980.

"I knew this would be the end of an era for the small shop owner, as well as the many Filipino families and African Americans who lived in the alleys South of Market.

"I wanted to acknowledge the beauty and viability of a community I could see was under siege. I made large color photographs to bring the place alive and emphasize the humanity of the neighborhood."

Photographs by Janet Delaney, poster for exhibition at 80 Langton Street, which was evicted from its Langton Street location and reopened on Folsom street as New Langton Arts in 1982.

FIVE ALARM NEIGHBORHOOD

Photographs and text from the July 10th San Francisco fire; a closer look at its effects on the neighborhood

Mary Gardner's kitchen. A 35 year resident, she was forced to move after the fire.

AUGUST 4–29, 1981

TUESDAY–SATURDAY, 11 AM TO 5 PM
RECEPTION: AUGUST 4, 6 TO 8 PM

Photographers:

**Janet Delaney, Connie Hatch
Barbara Martz/Bobby Adams
Jim Pomeroy, Bill Washburn**

Photo credit: Janet Delaney

80 LANGTON STREET, SAN FRANCISCO, 626-5416

Redevelopment?

Over 100 families lost their homes here . . .

Photograph by Connie Hatch

Connie Hatch:

"It was just a matter of time before a catastrophe of this magnitude would happen. Two fire stations that had serviced the South of Market had been closed. The fire broke out around 1 a.m. It was a whole city block. It took the Fire Department so long to get there. A hundred dwellings burned, and over 5,000 people were impacted. It was also a gay and leather community, and the newspaper articles were outrageous—describing the bath-houses, and the drugs used, and headlines about the whips and chains. Finally in a small article it was revealed as an arson fire—a disgruntled employee on the edge of insanity, a housepainter who lit some rags.

"The *Chronicle* was on a campaign to discredit the residents of the neighborhood—claiming that no decent people would live South of Market—therefore it was okay for the city to take it over."

"… And even without the fire, people are being forced out because of changes in the area. Figures crop up around 5,000 people who were being displaced. It's going to be too expensive for the working-class people to live here. It's happening all over San Francisco and in this area right now, rents are being raised outrageously, where the only people who can afford to live here, and maybe in San Francisco in the coming years, will be professional single white people, which is very unfortunate. It's taking away the identity of our city." —Laura Graham

Connie Hatch, The Changing Landscape South of Market, 5 Fremont, photograph with text, 1981

"Our intention was to weave the politics of displacement into the politics of authority that the city institutions have in collusion with big business."

Opening ceremonies, George Moscone Center, 1985. Photograph by Connie Hatch.

Priorities?

"The Survival Corner was across the street from what is now the Yerba Center for the Arts, on Mission and Third. The poorest people left in the neighborhood could eke out an existence by getting a burger there every other day. I drove by recently and saw that they are building luxury apartments on that spot. It's ironic to think of its history.

"I lived and photographed South of Market for ten years. I miss living in the city. I miss that feeling of clambering down the stairs and going out on the street. You're with a lot of other people doing the same thing. You felt like you were part of the industry of human effort. It's not an image, it's not a lifestyle, you're working with the world. You are weaving the fabric of your life into the fabric of the city and feeling that effort of the city is your effort too. I can't afford to live in San Francisco now, and I'm not sure if I could, it would feel the same."

Model of Mission Bay.

Hulk, Mission Bay.

A Real Estate History of the Avant-Garde

A Few Evictions

Mission Bay will be the biggest development ever in San Francisco. The linchpin of this 300-acre site will be a huge new biotechnology facility built by the University of California, San Francisco. In its 8.1 million square feet of workspace, Mission Bay will create 42,000 new jobs, mostly high-paying, but only 6,000 units of housing, few of them affordable.[1] This Catellus Corporation project will immediately displace the "vehicularly housed" community there, in what was long an abandoned railyard; it will make inroads on the scruffy houseboat community on Mission Creek—and some of those high-paid biotechnologists will start buying out Potrero Hill homes from under the residents, just as multimedia people are doing in the Mission. The worst-case scenario is historian Gray Brechin's: Mission Bay is a toxic landfill site that in an earthquake will liquefy, spilling biogoop everywhere. Brechin remarks, "The main business of San Francisco is increasing the value of land, and Willie Brown understands that."[2] Twenty years ago, when he was in state government, Brown

75

was the attorney for Mission Bay; as San Francisco's mayor he's completing a job he started on the other side of the fence. "We're now, frankly,
at the end of the rainbow," he declared when he pushed the plan through
the Board of Supervisors.[3] Catellus Corporation is a spin-off of Southern
Pacific, the "Octopus" of Frank Norris's novel, a vast and vastly corrupt
corporation that virtually ran California in its late nineteenth-century
heyday. Of that day, Oscar Lewis wrote, "Although the citizens had on
their side every important newspaper of the state save those frankly in
the pay of the Southern Pacific, efforts to remedy the situation were uni-
formly unsuccessful because of the railroad's control of the legislature,
of state regulatory bodies, of city and county governments, and, in many
cases, of the courts."[4] Mission Bay was its San Francisco railyard, and
Catellus has inherited the SP's position as the biggest nongovernmental
landholder in the city—and the state.

But there's more to San Francisco. The day I'm brooding on Mission Bay
I go to hear scientist and environmental activist Vandana Shiva give a talk
on what she calls "biopiracy," the attempt by biotech companies to create
genetically altered crops and then ensure markets for them by disrupting
the peasant economy and sustainable agriculture in her homeland, India.
Hilarious and scary, her exposition weaves together peasant uprisings, the
dangers of monoculture, scientific madness (with examples such as cab-
bages into which scorpion genes have been spliced) and corporate greed.
Brenda O'Sullivan from Modern Times Bookstore, one of the Mission's
longtime progressive institutions, is at the talk to provide the audience
with copies of Shiva's books, and the prolific and brilliant muralist Juana
Alicia is in the audience, too. Mission Bay and Southern Pacific represent
the central institutions of what Brechin calls "Imperial San Francisco,"
but Juana, Brenda and the University of San Francisco faculty who invited
Shiva represent the alternative institutions and traditions that are still a

force in the city. Juana and her frequent collaborator, Miranda Bergman, present Shiva with the drawing for an addition to their huge mural covering the Women's Building on Eighteenth Street near Valencia in the Mission. The addition portrays the four primary cereal grains eaten around the world and addresses genetic engineering and biodiversity. And, they tell Shiva, they're going to add her name to the list of feminist heroines painted on the building. "This part of the building used to be an Irish bar, but we have enough Irish bars and not enough childcare here, so it's a daycare center," says Juana. Shiva is delighted and says that she believes it's important that these issues become part of the culture.

Juana lures Miranda and me out to a Chinese restaurant in the Richmond District, where we continue our conversation. I tell her about Mission Bay and its probable effect on Potrero Hill's housing. "There goes my dream of coming back," she says. "I've painted this town, but I don't think I can live in it again. And Emmanuel says, 'Do you really want to live there? Everyone's gone.'" Juana tells me that she and her husband, the artist Emmanuel Montoya, were evicted from the Mission in the early 1990s, which is how she came to settle in a flat on a busy street in the Western Addition, only a few blocks from the Coltrane church, Rexroth's old digs, and the rest of that laden neighborhood that is still my neighborhood. But five years ago, in search of housing they could afford to buy, they moved to Berkeley (where they could not afford to buy now, she adds, as the inflationary ripple spreads outward). This is what makes the cultural raiding going on in the Mission matter. The Mission is home to the most significant concentration of murals in the country, and the murals represent an idea of art as part of everyday life, as a reinforcement of ethnic and sometimes feminist identity, a celebration of radical history, a populist art of the streets for those who use them. The murals mean that in moving through the streets, past churches and schools, Mission dwellers are moving through stories, past heroes, into legends and dreams.

The artists who came together in the early 1970s to make neighborhood culture organized against urban renewal when two stations of BART (Bay Area Rapid Transit, the intercity commuter train system) were put in on Mission Street as part of a plan to redevelop the neighborhood for downtown workers. Gentrification is, thirty years later, carrying out that redevelopment, with the delicate balance between the poor and the not-so-poor, the white and the nonwhite tipped by the multimedia invasion. One famous mural was painted over by the Cort Family developers, but it is not the extraction of the murals from the community but the community from the murals that poses the most serious threat. What Vandana Shiva said about the necessity of biodiversity could be equally applied to social diversity; it is what makes the city a thriving ecosystem, a garden in which the weeds sometimes bloom most brilliantly. Right now multimedia looks like monoculture. The expensive new businesses coming to the Mission include a plethora of restaurants and houseware and clothing stores, but bookstores, theaters, dance studios, galleries, "monoplex" movie houses and nonprofit activist organizations are shrinking, not multiplying, with this stage of gentrification.

Of course, progressive culture has its own history of displacements. As Juana obliquely mentioned, the Women's Building evicted the Dovre Club, the Irish bar set into one corner of the Women's Building like a chick under a mother hen's wing. This had been my vision of the Peaceable Kingdom: a wholesome, mural-covered matriarchy featuring a four-story-tall Rigoberta Menchú that could still accommodate old-fashioned masculine versions of liberation—for the Dovre Club, which opened in 1966, was filled with Irish nationalist iconography and had been host to many radicals before the main space became a Women's Building. A friend told me that when he used to participate in Starhawk's pagan Spiral

Dances in the Women's Building's gymnasium, he would occasionally duck out to watch a little football and have a shot of whiskey, and the world seemed to be in perfect harmony and balance. As several surviving bars testify, the Mission had, like the Castro, been a working-class Irish neighborhood, and when the Women's Building evicted the Dovre Club, the new order at least symbolically squeezed out the old. Not that it was a black and white story, for the Dovre successfully relocated, and some of its defenders were among San Francisco's most thuggish politicos. But the saga of the Dovre's displacement was a reminder that the progressive version of San Francisco also squeezes out people and institutions. Americans tend to mistake powerlessness for innocence, because both are without impact; it is because the Women's Building acquired power that it became able to evict. And Juana and Miranda will paint in panels about biodiversity where the Dovre once stood and a much-needed daycare center will open.

A Literary Eviction

Bohemia begins with an eviction. Or at least, *Scènes de la vie de bohème*, the book that introduced the word and the idea into popular consciousness does. "'If I understand the purport of this document,' said Schaunard re-reading an order to leave from the sheriff fixed to the wall, 'today at noon exactly I must have emptied these rooms and have put into the hands of Monsieur Bernard, my proprietor, a sum of seventy-five francs for three quarters rent, which he demands from me in very bad handwriting.'"[5] Henri Murger's stories about a quartet of starving Left Bank artists were published serially beginning in 1845, turned into a wildly successful play in 1849, and gathered together in 1851 as a bestselling book (Puccini's 1896 opera *La Bohème*, is, of course, based on Murger's work). Murger's stories about bohemia succeed in making poverty and its accompanying hunger,

The Black Cat restaurant, Montgomery
Street, early 1900s.

insecurity and occasional homelessness charming.
The musician-writer Schaunard is a feckless garret-
dweller who forgets about his eviction in a burst of
inspiration. "And Schaunard, half naked, sat down
at his piano. Having awakened the sleeping instru-
ment by a tempestuous barrage of chords—he com-
menced, all the while carrying on a monologue,
to pick out the melody which he had been search-
ing for so long."[6] On goes the romp; he sets out to
borrow the seventy-five francs, finds instead some
drinking companions, the philosopher Gustave and
the poet Rodolphe, drunkenly invites them back to
the home that is no longer his and meets Marcel, the
painter who has just moved in. More like the *Three
Musketeers* than *Les Misérables*, the episode continues
with the quartet forming the Bohemian Club and
Schaunard becoming Marcel's roommate. Commu-
nity has triumphed over capital. *Scènes* is an episodic book, each chapter
a picaresque adventure about love, friendship and scraping by. Murger
concludes this first tale with the assertion that these "heroes belong to a
class misjudged up to now, whose greatest fault is disorder; and yet they
can give as an excuse for this same disorder—it is a necessity which life
demands from them."[7]

The city is both the place where society is administered and where it is
transformed and challenged: it is both the Catellus Corporation operating a real-estate empire and the university bringing in Vandana Shiva to
urge a responsive audience to resist corporate power. This mix that cities
have traditionally provided makes them volatile, disorderly, creative and
necessary, and the mixing is brought about in various ways. In San Fran-

cisco nowadays, home-builders are obliged to set aside a certain number
of units as low-cost housing; in nineteenth-century Paris, low-cost housing was built into nearly every building. Before elevators, the top floor of
Parisian buildings was designed as a sort of residential hotel—the rooms
were called *chambres de bonne*, maids' rooms, in my day, when poor students and African immigrants filled them; they usually had a cold-water
sink and a communal toilet in the hallway (one cooked on a camping
stove; refrigeration was the windowsill in winter). This building style created a sort of integrated housing: a famous illustration of the nineteenth
century shows a cross-section of an apartment house with the bourgeoi-
sie in armchairs just above the ground-floor concierge and the inhabitants getting progressively poorer as it ascended to the wretches huddled
under the rooftop. Bohemia was the brownian motion of urban life; it
brought together people of different classes, was the incubator for those
who would rise through talent or sink through addiction, poverty, madness; was where the new would be tried out long before it would be found
palatable in the mainstream; was where memory was kept alive as paintings, stories, politics.

A Paris street c. 1865. Photograph by
Charles Marville, courtesy Robert Koch
Gallery, San Francisco.

George Sand's novel *Horace* gives a less prettified picture of bohemia
at the time of the 1830 revolution; among the novel's characters are dedicated painters and dilettantes, a slumming law-student squandering his
provincial family's funds and a dedicated peasant-revolutionary with great
sculptural talent, as well as a few sympathetically drawn grisettes. Grisettes were working-class women who formed liaisons of various dura-
tions with the varying classes of men who formed bohemia (because
the grisettes were seldom participants in creative life, save as muses and
singers, and because they were unable to move out of bohemia into the
salons, receptions and public arenas of the wealthy, bohemia's freedom
was largely male freedom—though Sand herself as a novelist and a lover

broke its rules to free herself). The excitement of Paris or of any great city is that of feeling one is in the center of things, a place where history is made, where things count. Paris still has this sense to perhaps a greater extent than any other city (though Beijing, Prague, Manila, Los Angeles and Seattle, have all had their moments).

Part of the fluidity of Parisian life comes from the way art has political weight, politics aesthetic merit, and figures such as Victor Hugo or Jean-Paul Sartre manage to act in both realms (something San Francisco has achieved in a very different way). Murger himself, the son of a conservative tailor, had gone to school with Eugene Pottier, who would write the *Internationale*. He remained apolitical while many of his circle—Baudelaire, Nadar, Courbet—became far more involved in the revolution of 1848. "Bohemia is the preface to the Hospital, the Academy, or the Morgue,"[8] Murger wrote after he had become a success. The consequences of his success seem strangely familiar now: the Cafe Momus he had made famous became a tourist trap that the artists vacated. Murger himself moved to a Right Bank apartment and then became a country gentleman in the forest of Fontainbleau. His partner opened an antique furniture store back in Paris. This general pattern of bohemia prevailed through the 1950s, at least. Bohemia moved around; at the turn of the twentieth century, it was in Montmartre more than the Left Bank; for a long time it was various versions of Greenwich Village; and it appeared in San Francisco, too, at various times and addresses.

Cities had a kind of porousness—like an old apartment impossible to seal against mice, cities were impossible to seal against artists, activists, dissidents and the poor. The remodeling of Paris between 1855 and 1870 by Baron von Haussmann under the command of Napoleon III is well-known for what it did to people's feelings, the poor and the old faubourgs. As Shelley Rice puts it in *Parisian Views*, "One of his first priorities had been to cut through and destroy the unhealthy, unsightly, and economically underprivileged areas that had been growing wildly and, in their horrific overpopulation, overtaking the heart of the town. By so doing the prefect hoped to roust the poor (who posed, he felt, a threat to both the city's health and the stability of its government) to the outlying banlieus."[9] Haussmannization encompassed urban renewal, but it did more; it sought to reinvent the relation of every citizen to the city. In modernizing the city, Haussmann and his emperor did some inarguably good things: they provided pure water and sewage systems. They did, with the building of boulevards, some debatable things: the boulevards increased circulation for citizens, commerce and, occasionally, soldiers, making the city more accessible for all purposes. And they erased the sites of peoples' memory and association: Baudelaire in "Le Cygne" and the brothers Goncourt in their famous journal entry bemoaned this architectural lobotomy. "My Paris, the Paris in which I was born, the Paris of the manners of 1830 to 1848, is vanishing, both materially and morally," the latter wrote. "I feel like a man merely passing through Paris, a traveller. I am foreign to that which is to come, to that which is, and a stranger to these new boulevards that go straight on, without meandering, without the adventures of perspective, implacably a straight line, without any of the atmosphere of Balzac's world, making one think of some American Babylon of the future. It is stupid to live in a time of growth; the soul is as uncomfortable as a body in a damp new house."[10]

It was homogenization, a loss of complexity, rather than absolute removal that most complained of. One of the key residential sites of early bohemia was the Impasse Doyenne, a quiet cul-de-sac overlooking a ruined church and weedy land in a city that had not yet rationalized and exploited all its space; Haussmannization erased the ruin, the Impasse and the weeds as it integrated this real estate into the Louvre and Tuiller-

ies that flank it. The new city was more rational, manageable, and commercial, but artists were more disoriented than displaced by Haussmannization. Many artists had private means—and though trust-fund artists are much denigrated nowadays, Baudelaire, Marcel Proust and Gertrude Stein were among their ranks. It was, too, partly a matter of the city remaining porous even after Haussmannization. New apartment buildings continued to supply *chambres de bonne*, and the poor and working-class neighborhoods endured. Though rents in the center of the city doubled between 1851 and 1857, it was the poorest who were most dramatically affected—and yet, as T. J. Clark puts it, "Paris in 1870, for all Haussmann's alterations, was still overwhelmingly working class."[11] The city remained a great capital for poetry and insurrection, and the boulevards and the smart new cafés and shops inspired painters, novelists and poets as, say, housing projects and urban freeways did not in the era of Robert Moses, and as global capitalism's chain stores and corporate logos probably will not (though skyscrapers had their moment early in the twentieth century). Perhaps it is that Paris under Haussmann could afford to lose far more than a modern American city, after so many cycles of erasure and homogenization.

Bohemian Territories

The idea of bohemia caught on quickly. Before the end of the Civil War, Ada Clare, the "Queen of Bohemia," arrived in San Francisco from Paris via New York and stayed to become a local luminary and a contributor to the literary magazine *The Golden Era*.[12] In 1872, San Francisco's Bohemian Club was founded by journalists and for the rest of the century included artists and writers. San Francisco had a lot of resident writers in those years: Mark Twain, Bret Harte, Ambrose Bierce, Joaquin Miller, Gertrude Atherton, Frank Norris, Ina Coolbrith, Jack London (born south of Market Street), and, peripherally, John Muir. Among those who stayed more briefly in the decades before the First World War were the great champion of Native American rights Helen Hunt Jackson, Robert Louis Stevenson, Mary Austin, Jaime de Angulo and Margaret Anderson. Oscar Wilde, who visited in 1882, remarked, "It is an odd thing, but anyone who disappears is said to be seen in San Francisco. It must be a delightful city and possess all the attractions of the next world."[13] By most accounts, it was indeed a marvelous city that had yet to produce great writers but that nevertheless provided a sense of great possibility. Photography was the medium that most flourished here early on, perhaps because a new medium needed a new locale: in the nineteenth century Carleton Watkins and Eadweard Muybridge generated the major landscape photographs of the age; in the twentieth, Ansel Adams, Imogen Cunningham

The Black Cat, 1930s. Photograph by Sam Cherry.

and their peers in San Francisco (and Edward Weston in Carmel) founded the f.64 group that revolutionized the medium. Few San Francisco painters before 1945 were better than pleasant, but the place certainly had artists—Rexroth estimated that there were 700 of them in 1934, on the eve of the city's General Strike, and in 1935 the San Francisco Museum of Art became the country's second museum devoted to modern art (though the word "modern" was added to its title decades later).

Diego Rivera writes of the enormous significance the place had for Frida Kahlo, whom he had married just before they embarked for San Francisco in 1930, "Frida told me she had dreamed for years about going to San Francisco.... En route to San Francisco, Frida surprised me with a gift of a portrait of herself which she had recently completed. Its background was an unfamiliar city skyline.... When we arrived in San Francisco, I was almost frightened to realize that her imagined city was the very one we were now seeing for the first time."[14] Rivera and Kahlo arrived in 1930 and settled into the painter Peter Stackpole's Montgomery Block studio. Built in 1852, the Montgomery Block had once been the financial headquarters of San Francisco and, at four stories, the tallest building west of the Mississippi; when business moved away from the location, it was turned into dozens of cheap artists' studios at the center of a lively artists' community (in *Literary San Francisco*, Nancy Peters writes that more than two thousand artists and writers lived there over the years). By 1959, business had returned to the area, and the Monkey Block, as it was nicknamed, was demolished to build the high-rise Transamerica Pyramid, San Francisco's most visible architectural mistake.

Rivera had come to paint murals commissioned by members of the Bohemian Club, which had already changed radically since its founding (though it was not yet the oligarchical fraternity it would become by the 1980s, when Ronald Reagan's California cabinet supplied its most visible members). The Bohemian Club and Rivera together illuminate some of the contradictions visual art has yet to iron out. At the Bohemian Club, as one artist put it, "In the beginning, rich men were absolutely barred, unless they had something of the elements of true Bohemian-

OLD MONTGOMERY BLOCK 1-12-59

ism.... Things have changed; now the simply rich become members because it is fashionable.... The poor artist or literary man gets in, by hook or by crook, because he thinks he may be able to sell some of his brains to the merely rich."[15] Gentrification of a sort had taken over the Bohemian Club, though some astute and daring patrons remained within its ranks, notably Albert Bender, an Irish immigrant become insurance mogul, who obtained Rivera's visa and initiated Rivera's two commissions. One was for the California School of Fine Arts (now the San Francisco Art Institute); the other was for the Pacific Stock Exchange.

That a famously communist painter should go to work painting the lunchroom of a stock exchange says something about the tendencies of much visual art. Those who produce enormously expensive unique objects almost inevitably produce them for a premodern patronage economy. Medici or Vatican, Vatican or Medici, rich patrons and powerful institutions are the available choices for such artists, which often limits not only what they can say—as Rivera found when he went to work for a Rockefeller—but whom they can say it to. Nowadays, most arts nonprofits depend on foundation and federal support, which dilutes but hardly does away with these issues. The most radical visual artists have focused not only on making statements but making means of display and distribution that revise or subvert this scenario. Reproducible media like photography and printmaking can be far more economically accessible or even, like writing, find their true home in mass-produced books. Though writers in the eighteenth century sold subscriptions and earlier writers sought patrons, their product was for a far wider audience than the patron or the subscribers. The publisher's advance replaced the subscription, and books have generally been relatively cheap mass-market products dependent on a popular rather than a powerful audience. Dance, music, theater have varying audiences and spatial needs, but their essential immateriality and performative quality means that they are for a group audience, a public, at least. And writers and performers can usually live in ordinary circumstances; visual artmaking requires a lot of individual work space, which is why visual art is the most high-profile and most endangered genre in San Francisco—though Susan Miller of New Langton Arts remarks that artwork is getting smaller as artists more and more often work in bedrooms or at kitchen tables, instead of the big spaces that brought us the big art of the 1970s and 1980s. The miniaturist Tino Rodriguez told me he paints in the bathroom in the Mission District flat he shares with roommates.

Bob Kaufman reading from his first book at the Coffee Gallery, photographer Imogen Cunningham in audience, c. 1959. Photograph by C. J. Snyder; courtesy Shaping San Francisco.

Visual art has two audiences, those who will look at it in public and semi-public spaces—museums, lobbies, galleries—and those who will actually buy it. Since the 1950s adventurous artists have been pursuing what Lucy Lippard calls "the dematerialization of the art object," making ephemeral, site-specific, public, performance, film- and video-based and outdoor works that were at least initially not easily moved into the marketplace. Recently a number of artists have taken up the Internet as an immaterial arena for art (while others have taken it up as a salesroom). But great numbers of artists continue to make objects priced in the thousands and tens of thousands of dollars to be sold to patrons and collectors in an economic system that predates the Renaissance. That making extremely expensive objects requires cultivating connections with the rich is something that many artists swallow without having tasted. And the rich often use art as a sort of identity-laundering scheme. For example, San Francisco's Haas family, which owns the Levi-Strauss clothing company, has had in recent years a fairly hideous labor record but a glorious patronage one, and the family foundations' donations to the arts are far more visible than, say, the El Paso seamstresses who became destitute when their jobs were sent across the border in the early 1990s. The artist Hans Haacke once demonstrated how incisively an artist can bite the feeding hand with his Guggenheim Museum exhibition documenting the slum real estate holdings of museum board members. The show was canceled, but it and its information went down in history anyway. Similarly, Ira Nowinski has had trouble showing and publishing his Yerba Buena documentary work because the board members and patrons of local visual-arts organizations often have ties to the place's development.

Rivera's *Allegory of California* mural in the Pacific Stock Exchange can be seen as a political statement, if not a very dangerous one: it depicts the physical activities and material resources that were then the primary sources of the state's wealth: mining, agriculture, industry. At the California School of Fine Arts, the mural was titled *Making a Fresco, Showing the Building of a City*, and its side panels depicted the industrial labors one might expect—a woman architect, steelworkers, carpenters. But at the center, Rivera painted a scaffold on which artists were painting a huge worker, suggesting that though workers built the city, artists built the worker—that is, that they constructed the very ideas and identities on which class, work, city life are based, a fitting assertion for an art school that has sent generations of subversives out into the world. Rivera galvanized the local mural scene, and during the New Deal several San Francisco sites—notably Coit Tower on Telegraph Hill—received overtly political murals and generated a fair-sized controversy (more recent mural projects tend to be supported by communities and progressive nonprofits,

far more democratic patrons to deal with). Kahlo flourished in San Francisco and painted a number of portraits, including a marriage portrait of
herself with Rivera that Bender donated to the San Francisco Museum of
Modern Art, where it is still on display. The Montgomery Block became
the Transamerica Pyramid, but bohemia had moved on.

A Painter's Eviction

If f.64 was the first, then California's second significant avant-garde art
movement began in the 1950s when several visual artists tied to the Beat
poets gathered in San Francisco (Bay Area Figurative painting, a revolt
against abstract-expressionism that could also be counted as a significant
movement, began about the same time, and figures such as Joan Brown
and David Park had ties to both communities). My first book was on
Bruce Conner, Jay DeFeo and her husband, Wally Hedrick, Jess, Wallace
Berman, and George Herms, six visual artists who were closely tied to
the Beat poets and to the gestation of experimental film and alternative
culture in California, and writing it in the already-lousy-for-tenants late
1980s I came to appreciate how much a copious supply of cheap housing
contributed to the era's sense of freedom. The artists of the era could
live as they wished, for there always seemed to be some place to go when
the money ran out or the landlord objected. The literal and psychological mobility of those times is antithetical to the immobilizing effect of
scarcity and fear nowadays. "San Francisco was a hotbed of liberalism
and Pacific Coastal rim ideas and environmental consciousness at its early
stages and a place where one could live in a lovely apartment with a
view and low rent that an artist might be able to afford," recalls the poet
Michael McClure, who was close to many of the artists.[16]

Those artists recognized that there was no art market on the West
Coast, and many of them had consciously chosen to reject New York

and any chance at commercial success in favor of the low pressure and wide-open possibilities San Francisco represented. Many recognized that in order to make art, they needed to make a culture in which their art was possible, and so the 1950s saw a succession of artist-run galleries, publications and community-making endeavors. Walter Benjamin's comment, "Rather than ask, 'What is the *attitude* of a work of art to the relations of production of its time?' I should like to ask, 'What is its *position* in them?'" is germane, for here artists made work that was sometimes overtly political—dealing with the death penalty and the Vietnam War, as well as divergent communal identities—but they also created a culture that was an alternative to the patronage economy and the passivity of those waiting for support.[17] Jess and his partner, Robert Duncan—poet, anarchist and publicly gay man—ran the King Ubu Gallery for a year, and in 1954 the Six Gallery, run by four artists and two poets, took over Ubu's upper Fillmore Street site in what was not yet an upscale neighborhood (it took its name from the six who founded it—gay poets Jack Spicer and John Allen Ryan, African-American artist Hayward King, and the painters Deborah Remington, David Simpson and Hedrick, though the Six eventually came to have dozens of dues-paying members). Later Conner was instrumental in launching the Batman Gallery and, with filmmaker Larry Jordan, an experimental film society, while Wallace Berman functioned as a publisher, exhibitor, salon host and general fomenter of connections and provider of support. The most famous event of the era, the great watershed in American art, was Allen Ginsberg's 1955 reading of *Howl* at the Six—famous in part because it is a central scene in Jack Kerouac's *Dharma Bums*. Less famous are the details that five other poets, including McClure and Gary Snyder read, that those two read poetry that was already environmentalist, that Rexroth was the master of ceremonies, and that it all transpired in the Six Gallery. An artists' collective had supplied the space in which poetry triumphed. Far more seriously than in *Scènes de la vie bohème*, community had triumphed over capitalism. The 1950s saw both the "San Francisco Renaissance" in poetry and the so-called Beats open up the possibilities of American literature, both stylistically and politically, and while the trio of official Beats were Eastern, both Ginsberg and Kerouac found liberation and confirmation in San Francisco.

Conner's black and white film *The White Rose* documents the 1964 removal of Jay DeFeo's monumental one-ton painting *The Rose* from her long-term home by a group of unusually priestly looking moving men. The seven-minute movie is about many things: the artist's passionate commitment to this work, the mandala-like spiritual icon the painting had become, the melancholy end of the intricate relationship between artist, home, and art. But at a fundamental level the film is about eviction. In the mid-1950s, DeFeo and many other artists and poets had moved into the spacious flats at 2322 Fillmore Street in what was then the edge of the Fillmore District and is now called Lower Pacific Heights, but in 1964 her rent was raised from $65 to $300 a month and she was forced to move. I asked Michael McClure why North Beach has always been associated with the Beats when the majority of them lived elsewhere—particularly in the Western Addition, on the edges of the city's main African-American neighborhood. He told me, "North Beach was like a reservation in which there was a free space for bohemians and oddballs of all stripes to meet in between the Italian and the Chinese districts in what was still a remarkably inexpensive part of town with lots of [residential] hotels. A lot of those very constructive people got out of there in '56 or '57 when the 'beatnik' thing started—because of the tour buses—and the obvious place to go was the Western Addition."[18]

Poster for King Ubu Gallery, 3119 Fillmore Street, 1953. Courtesy San Francisco Museum of Modern Art Library.

Conner has since become celebrated as a filmmaker as well as an artist; a huge exhibition of his work opened at the Walker Art Center in late 1999 and traveled to three other major American museums in 2000. I asked him to recall his beginnings in San Francisco, and he told me the rent he and his bride Jean Sandstedt Conner paid in their first place on Jackson Street, near Fillmore, was $65 a month in 1957. But, he admonished me, coming up with that sum was "not so easy if you were making one penny over minimum wage. I was working as a movie usher and Jean was working at a concession stand. She was also getting paid a dollar and one cent per hour.... We were living on Jackson Street in this three-room thing and Wallace Berman and Shirley [Berman] moved in down the street about three months after we moved in, about six or seven houses east of us on that block." Artists lived much more modestly then than now, he added. "We'd eat out once a month at the cheapest Chinese restaurant we could find and get about the least expensive thing that was on the menu. The rest of time we were eating hot dogs and peanut butter sandwiches." As for housing, "It was easy to evict people but it was easy to find another a place. My rent went up to $85 ... I had to move out because we couldn't afford it, and at the same time Wallace and Shirley's rent went up from $65 to $125—they *really* didn't want them there. So I moved over to 1205 Oak Street and Wallace and Shirley and [their son] Tosh moved over to Alamo Square. Then we didn't have any real problems...."[19] They had moved from the northern to the southern edge of the Western Addition, near what would become known as the Haight-Ashbury.

Meanwhile, the 2322 Fillmore Building became a sort of latter-day Bateau Lavoir—the building in which Picasso and many of his peers lived during their starving-in-Montmartre phase. McClure and his family, gallerist James Newman, painter Sonia Gechtoff, and later the painters Joan Brown and Bill Brown lived at 2322 Fillmore as neighbors and friends of

DeFeo and Wally Hedrick. "We were enjoying the Black stores, the Black ambience, the Black music," recalls McClure. "We had our faces towards them but our butts towards Pacific Heights."[20] DeFeo had worked on her painting *The Rose* for several years, eventually installing it in the bay window of the front room of her flat, which she used as a studio. The painting and her commitment to it became legendary, and her peers speak of DeFeo with an awe no one else elicited. The Rose came to weigh about a ton as the paint built up to become several inches thick, and the floor around it was, recalls Bruce, so layered with paint that walking on it was like walking on the back of a whale. The house had become magical and slightly sinister, an extension of the painting that was so much an extension of the artist. *The White Rose* documents the severing of each from each, with Miles Davis's "Sketches in Spain" as a soundtrack that underscores the melancholy of the moment. DeFeo, who died in Oakland in 1989, never lived in San Francisco again.

Still of Jay DeFeo from *The White Rose* by Bruce Conner, 16mm black and white film, 1967. DeFeo is sitting in the hole cut into the wall of her apartment to remove *The Rose*. Courtesy of Bruce Conner.

And a Wave of Displacement

Any accurate history of the urban avant-gardes and bohemias must be in part a history of urban real estate and economics generally. Several factors made the postwar era peculiarly encouraging for bohemias and countercultures. Postwar affluence was, unlike today's boom, widely distributed. Veterans were eligible both for home loans—which accelerated the expansion of suburbia, making cities even more available to artists—and for the GI Bill, which fueled, so to speak, the expansion of the intelligentsia. As Richard Candida Smith writes in his history of California artists and writers, *Utopia and Dissent*, "Between 1945 and 1957 two and a quarter million veterans attended college-level schools under the GI Bill (65,000 were women). By 1947 the total college enrollment in the United States had jumped 75 percent over the prewar record. . . . Educators were surprised by the educational choices veterans made. The assumption that their primary goal would be to learn practical skills was overturned when veterans who attended college-level institutions preferred liberal arts education over professional training."[21]

UC Berkeley geographer Richard Walker describes the effects of these forces locally: "The central city was in the dumps. Most of the action was going out to the suburbs, creating space for people to come in. Normally the model was that poor African Americans from the South and immigrants came into these city neighborhoods. In San Francisco there wasn't a mass labor demand for the poor, so bohemians could come in and set up shop. It was a boom, but it was a boom with a difference, a boom with a social support system. There was money flowing to a lot of people in new ways and so it helped create a youth culture, a culture of leisure, and an alternative bohemian culture, too."[22] Elsewhere he writes, "Prosperity worked its magic more effectively as long as rents remained low enough to allow artists, refugees, and those outside the mainstream to survive, if not prosper, in the inner city. The long slump in central-city investment due to depression, war, and suburbanization had left property markets relatively untouched for two decades. The confluence of economic growth without property speculation through the 1950s was ideal for nurturing the countercultures that mushroomed in San Francisco. Conversely, the heating up of real estate in the seventies and eighties drove out many of the marginals; as old commercial space disappeared, the affluent crowded into gentrifying neighborhoods. . . ."²³ DeFeo's eviction came ten years before the real-estate boom started changing the possibilities for artists, though urban renewal was in full swing not far south of her on Fillmore Street. What Conner's film captures is the melancholy of displacement of an individual, not the politics of mass displacement.

Between the eviction and the boom came the counterculture, and nowhere is the real estate foundation of culture more evident than in the Haight Ashbury, circa 1967–1971. Or so Calvin Welch, who was there then—and still is now—told me. I walked over from my home not far from where Conner, Rexroth and Berman settled to 409 House, a block and a half from the intersection of Haight and Ashbury Streets. It's a Victorian building housing several progressive outfits, and from it Welch has operated as an affordable housing activist since the 1970s, currently as director of the Council of Community Housing Organizations (among other accomplishments, he was a coauthor of Proposition M). Imposing and amused, Welch sat in a stark back office in front of a computer whose screen switched back and forth from a "Lewis and Clark" title to a map of the United States in 1803, when the whole huge swath of California and the far west was still Spain's, soon to be Mexico's. One side of the bay window had ivy curtaining it and a tendril coming through the gap between upper and lower sashes. The other looked out onto the neighbor's backyard, and the neighbor himself—a lean, aged man in bike shorts and a truss with an upper body lightly covered in gray hair—kept coming into view to pick up a few more bricks and move them out of sight in the verdant garden. Aerial photographs of Yerba Buena Center and the blueprint for Mission Bay were tacked to the wall.

Hippies, Welch told me, depressed housing prices when they arrived, and they chased out the African Americans who had relocated to the Haight from the adjoining Western Addition. What looked like a nice student couple would rent a place, and then forty hippies would move in, and they'd stop paying rent and scandalize the neighbors. "The essence of the hippie was to do no work, so there was no connection to an economy except the barter economy or the rough cash economy of selling dope.... Hippie girls supported whole communes doing pornography, but that was a very tiny thing. The overwhelming majority of hippies lived off welfare or checks from home."[24] Dozens of Haight-Ashbury households paid no rent at all—and this confirmed what I, born on the baby-boom/ Generation X cusp had always suspected: that the widespread revolutionary spirit of the sixties was made possible by an economy so expansive that its bounty spilled over onto the middle-class kids who didn't participate in it, that freedom was, so to speak, more affordable then, the margins far wider and more inviting than ever before or since.

By 1977, everything was different. There had been a huge change in the economy; wages had started to flatten out as inflation skyrocketed, places like San Francisco had undergone huge increases in housing prices, and the fat of the land had been pretty much eaten up. Politics were washed up between the failures of sixties-style revolution and the 1980s surge of non-violent direct action around nuclear issues, the wars in Central America, human rights and the environment. As David Antin, who had flourished as a young artist in New York's easy 1950s housing climate, put it in a 1988 lecture at the San Francisco Art Institute, "Every city in the United States is suffering from real estate inflation, which means that young people going to the city to make it can't afford to live the way artists used to live.... It contributes to an enormous anxiety for the young, who are the people who become artists in an environment where other people are artists. They go there and they can't survive there. The streets are filled with people who can't find places to live because it's too expensive to live.... It seems to me this economic disaster of inflation and the disastrous, dire effect upon the young was being felt in the 1970s in every city that was a significant city where you could go to be an artist. I remember it as the appearance of punk—that is, the punk sensibility seemed to emanate from a lot of kids who wanted to make meaningful things some way or another under conditions that were very unlivable, surrounded by other people who found it unlivable. Now it may not be true that the country is in terrible shape, but when you're in those conditions that's what the country feels like. If you're having a very hard time and all your friends are having a very hard time, it feels like the world is in bad shape."[25]

"No future," sang the Sex Pistols from London. "We're desperate," chorused X from L.A., "Get used to it." Punk rock took place among the ruins—among the ruins of post-industrial cities before the new consumer-and-capital booms, among the ruins of modernism's faith in the future, among the ruins of the sixties' hubris and idealism, among the ruins of an economy that had set an older generation free. South of Market were the abandoned Hamms beer vats where Survival Research Labs, a group whose machines performed their rites of violence and entropy, once performed—a huge cinderblock Costco now occupies the site—and another place just known as The Beer Vats housed rehearsal studios and artists then. Punk managed to revive anarchy as a political philosophy and to articulate an insurrection more akin to the Beats than the hippies, as well as to provide a musical medium for adolescent angst and revolt that soon pervaded the garages and college radio stations of the country. By the 1980s, squatting had become part of punk-rock culture, because affordable, let alone free, housing wasn't available. In the Reagan era, the apocalypse seemed near and the options seemed limited.

The housing crises hit New York hardest in the 1980s. Probably the first time artists had ever been involved in gentrification in any significant way was in SoHo, where hordes of artists had moved in the 1960s and 1970s, only to find it become first fashionable and then prohibitively expensive by the 1980s. It was the first time that class identities were so reshuffled that wealthier citizens wanted to live like artists in that neighborhood, rather than just buy their work, see versions of their lives onstage, or drink in their cafes. I am not sure that artists should be held responsible for gentrification; it is not necessarily their fault that wealthy professionals follow their lead. After all, creeps tend to follow teenage girls around, but teenage girls neither create nor encourage them. Another way to put it is: redevelopment is like an oil spill, with a single cause and a responsible party; gentrification is like air pollution, a lot of unlinked individuals make contributions whose effect is only cumulatively disastrous. One can blame artists and drivers for those cumulative effects, but such effects are not their intention. Two of San Francisco's most significant artists—Jess and David Ireland—moved to the heart of the Mission thirty-five and twenty-five years ago, respectively, and live there still; it is clearly not talented individual artists but the widespread ambience created by cafés, nightclubs, galleries and those who hang out in them—by a visible bohemia, along with "lifestyle" commodities—that seeds gentrification. This is why North Beach, with its cafés and bars, is famous for a Beat bohemia that was largely elsewhere and why the Haight is still selling psychedelia to kids born in the 1980s. What is the counter-argument: should artists and activists redline nonwhite and poor neighborhoods; and if so, where should they look for affordable housing? The larger economic forces that produce those able to gentrify are culpable parties, along with cities that leave housing issues almost entirely to the free market, even when booms produce epics of social darwinist struggle over housing.

As SoHo and then the Lower East Side were gentrifying, some fought back. There were the famous battles of Tompkins Square over whether the homeless could continue to camp there, and a plethora of graffiti and anti-gentrification posters made the struggle more visible. During the 1980s, there was a surge of visual art with political content and of public art that sought to be a form of political intervention (and of "political-flavored art," in which politics is more a credential than a commitment); many of the individuals who emerged then remain active into the present, but the sense of a movement is gone. Perhaps what's gone is that world-changing hubris, though a number of artists moved into a number of social arenas to continue effecting change without so many banners and trumpets. In the early 1980s, other New York artists were fighting a different kind of battle to ensure their ability to stay—a struggle for legislation giving artists special rights and roles. For example, the Department of Cultural Affairs' artists' certification program legalized the conversion of industrial buildings into artists' living and working space, and the Artist Home Ownership Program helped some artists make the transition from renting to owning. By the late 1980s, the role of artists in gentrification and the merits of artists being given special status were under discussion in New York. Artists didn't seem to be numerous or wealthy enough to create significant displacement, but they were glamorous enough to attract it. (The artist Martha Rosler's 1988 anthology *If You Lived Here: The City in Art, Theory, and Social Activism* documents the debates then about homelessness, housing and artists' place in New York's space and in its politics.) In San Francisco, artists inspired by the Manhattan example fought for and won the "live/work" ordinance, the biggest Trojan horse artists ever dragged into a city. Like the New York certification program, it was intended to legitimize artists converting industrial space into live-in studios (and a tale could be told about industries that were leaving the inner-city cores and about how a whole aesthetic and scale developed out

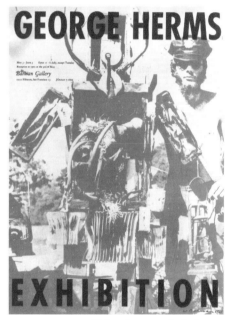

Wallace Berman, poster for George Herms' show at the Batman Gallery, 2222 Fillmore Street, San Francisco, 1961. © Estate of Wallace Berman. Courtesy L.A. Louver Gallery, Venice, Calif.

of artists moving into those spaces). San Francisco artists managed to get a measure passed that allowed them to build or convert in regions zoned for industry, to circumvent building codes, and to avoid affordable housing stipulations and a significant portion of school taxes. Once again some visual artists had become confused about their relationship to wealth and to poverty, only this time the results were practical and pervasive.

Joan Holden of the San Francisco Mime Troupe and the Coalition on Jobs, Art and Housing told me, "The affordable housing people said, 'Watch out—you're creating a bonanza for developers.'"[26] Debra Walker, an artist who has lived in a nonprofit-owned artists' building for fifteen years and participated in housing politics nearly as long, had harsher things to say about the 1988 live/work ordinance: "Artists in City Hall were adamant that they did not want to be defined, so not only did we ask for special housing or special zoning, we refused to be part of any solution for enforcement. It really was the artists who screwed themselves on this, because artists didn't want to be defined. I don't think the answer is to take a group of people and make special housing for them. If live/work had to be affordable housing, it would've been a lot more successful and it [the regulations] would have been harder to get around. You have got to take speculation out of things like this or you lose. In the mid-1990s, I noticed a lot more lofts going up and I went to look at them and said, these are not for artists.... Shortly thereafter there was this proliferation of lofts and the prices were starting going up and businesses were started to get dislocated, and all of a sudden it was like this wild thing. Mortgage companies started giving residential loans for lofts. After that anybody could buy one, so that was really what created the whole building boom, plus there was a need. Multimedia was just starting to come in." Walker first noticed the loft problem because she paints cityscapes: looking at the city closely led her to recognize its transformation early and take political action.

Live/work spaces have become infamous as cheaply built condominiums at sky-high prices almost no artist can afford. From near downtown to the city's poorest southern reaches, these angular modernist structures with glaring walls of glass pop up between industrial buildings, old Victorians and other older buildings, directly displacing numerous small businesses. According to the Coalition on Jobs, Art and Housing, "The Planning Department's own studies show that not protecting industrial areas will cost the City 13,000–27,000 jobs in: production, distribution, auto repair, garment manufacturing, delivery services, printing and moving companies. These jobs must stay in the City to support industries like finance, multimedia, real estate, and tourism. The jobs at stake are stable, low-skill, high-wage jobs essential to a thriving economy."[28] Several hundred jobs already lost can be traced directly to the replacement of workplaces by live/work condos; many other small businesses have been forced to relocate or close because the new neighbors just wanted their neighborhood to *look* industrial, not *be* industrial. The newcomer neighbors have objected to longstanding activities ranging from meatpacking plants to a school that funds teaching English to immigrants by holding big dances on weekends. The *San Francisco Examiner* reports, "Andrew Wood, director of the ODC Theater, a dance performance venue in the Mission, noted that it's not the loft developers who do the evicting, but the property owners who sell them the land. 'All the landlords in this part of The City are being sent letters saying, "Do you know you're sitting on a gold mine? All you have to do is get the existing tenants out and then we'll buy from you,"' Wood said, 'ODC is a landowner so we get these letters all the time.' His dance theater, which has been at 17th and Shotwell Streets for twenty years, fears it will be the target of complaints about noise if a proposed loft project gains approval to go up next door."[29] Others argue that live/work spaces enlarge the housing supply, taking at least a few upscale home purchasers out of the competition for existing housing, but almost none are built on vacant sites.

Holden and Walker insist on the necessity of seeing artists as part of a larger community rather than as a separate group entitled to special treatment—thus their active roles in the Coalition on Jobs, Art and Housing and Walker's appointment to the city's Building Inspection Commission. In her studio filled with cityscapes and botanical paintings, Walker tells me, "I get this all the time: 'I don't have time to be involved. I don't have the energy, I need to be doing my art,' and God love 'em, soon they will not have time and space for that either, because they will be a victim of their inaction. People need to do something—it's time, and if not us who? I think that artists will either leave or they'll become part of the battle. I think that what's happening is that you're displacing people who don't have options, people who want to stay in San Francisco and don't have the options to go somewhere else, and the more you do that the more angry people are going to get. I think there's going to be a lot of revolution, more so than we've seen. Unless we come together we will fall apart—artists tend to use their own demanding work as an excuse to not be involved, and I want to shake them to wake them up. Not only are we stupid—we helped create the problem in the first place—but now we can't even come together to agree on a way to solve it. I'm part of organizations that include the labor movement and affordable housing, and there is so much anger at the arts community—as the privileged, the gateopeners, the voluntary poor. Artists get to be up there with the wealthy—but what kind of freedom is that? We have to get down in the trenches and fight with the other people who are on our side, align ourselves with the unions, with the affordable housing people, with the people *in* the affordable housing."[30]

Now the future is supposed to be bright and capitalistic, but gaining admission to that future is getting harder. Taking the scenic bohemian detour makes it harder yet. In 1957, Bruce and Jean Conner's rent represented 65 hours of minimum-wage work split between two people. At today's minimum wage of $5.50 an hour, an apartment for two would have to cost $357.50 a month to be comparable; in fact, the average San Francisco apartment rented for $1,861 in early 1999, representing instead five times as much work—324 hours at the minimum wage, nearly all the pretax earnings of two fulltime minimum-wage workers.[31] The postwar boom was radically inclusive, but the new boom is as radically exclusive.

A Pending Eviction

In the Taiwanese restaurant after Vandana Shiva's talk, I tell Juana Alicia that it looks like the artist René Yanez is going to lose his home. "That's like evicting the history of the Mission," Juana says, adding that the artist Yolanda Lopez lives in the same building and will face the same threat. Yanez told me that he came here from Oakland in 1970 because San Francisco was a better place for the arts. He was working with the neighborhood arts program here—and in those days, he said, Emmy Lou Packard was the head of the Arts Commission. Packard had been Diego Rivera's assistant, and so she bridged two eras of mural movements. Yanez thus forms a strong link in a chain going back from Packard to Rivera to the Bohemian Club to the nineteenth century and forward through the younger artists he has fostered as a teacher and a catalyst. In the Mission, Yanez helped start Galería de la Raza in 1970, then later on the Latino performance/comedy group Culture Clash, and he remains active as an artist and a performer.

The Mission has been as dense in artistic activity as any neighborhood could be, and when the Day of the Dead/Dia de los Muertes procession full of artists' puppets and props would leave the Galleria to wind through

Balmy Alley, which had more than thirty murals dealing with the conflicts and cultures in Central America, the excitement, the possibilities, the connections were intoxicating. But when I met with Yanez, he was caught up in another matter entirely. The city, he told me, had just seized his landlord's building after a newcomer next-door neighbor—a white artist—had turned him in for having an illegal apartment that housed a family of undocumented immigrants. Yanez had been in the building for twenty-two years and feared it would be sold; he liked his aged Irish landlord, who represented an even earlier era of Mission ethnic history, and was trying to help him struggle out of the legal swamp. "They're circling like sharks," he said of the speculators who had advance notice of the building's uncertain status. Like so many San Franciscans, Yanez believes that if he loses his current perch, he will have to leave the city, and he doesn't know where he will go. There is still an appetite for the culture he makes—but the forces in California that a few years back in a bleaker economy attacked Latinos as illegals now just wanted their locations: "They want to 'improve' the neighborhood, and we're in the way."

Before he left town to take a job at New York's Whitney Museum, Bay Area curator Larry Rinder described his vision of the arts in San Francisco in twenty years. "San Francisco in 2020 is going to become a city of presentation without creation—much on the model of what we see in a place like Washington, D.C., now, where you have really premier centers for presentation like the National Gallery and the Kennedy Center, but very little in terms of vital, grassroots creative practice. In Washington because no artist would want to live there, and here because no artist will be able to afford to live here. The large-scale organizations will survive by booking only the most high-profile exhibitions and performances, and I think there will be relatively little room for experimentation or innovation.... I think you'll see very little of the down and dirty grassroots creativity that you need for a city to feel like an active and vital cultural center. The small- and medium-sized arts organizations will have folded unless they retool to cater to segments of the tourist community."[32] A city of presentation without creation defeats the essential purpose of radical art: to make art an invitation to join in rather than just to look on, to give voice to the unheard, to engender conversation about the meaning of the lives being led all around us, to build a vital relationship between artists and public. Many artists here work as teachers, and they teach not only skills and craft traditions, but critical thinking, independence from mainstream institutions and media, and alternative histories. To paint murals dealing with biotechnology and the basic grains on the walls of a daycare center means, in a small way, that those who grow up seeing them may better understand the relationship between the tortillas and artisan loaves being sold down the street, the biotech firms across town, the agricultural workers somewhere unseen and the market forces shaping our lives. To have community murals requires both muralists and a community.

In the future, there may be very few artists not because the urge stirred up during the postwar era has died down, but because the circumstances in which art can be made are disappearing. Cities will no longer be porous; the dissenters will no longer have a niche in them. On my most cheerful days I imagine an outmigration of artists to the small towns they can afford, a sort of unofficial artist-in-residence program throughout the nation's outback, one that will give rise to a populist art identified with the overlooked populations of small towns, reservations, remote places, resource-industry workers—something a little like 1930s regionalism (without the WPA to underwrite it, of course). On my least cheerful ones, I imagine a nation in which those who have something to say have nowhere effective to say it. At the end of 1999, I went to Seattle to protest the World Trade Organization and, from where my bohemian friends—

housing activists, radical photojournalists, sex activists—managed to buy homes while they still could, it took far longer to reach downtown than it did a few years ago when they rented in now-gentrified-by-computer-money Capital Hill. Political participation, along with access to the main museum, library and bookstores, had become a little less convenient; it could get inconceivably more so, and the Internet isn't going to make up for that. Haussmann sent the poor to the politically and culturally ineffectual outskirts, and so does the new gentrification.

It may be that the idea of a mass culture of bohemia was just possible during the period of postwar affluence, that the GI bill and cheap rents created a large-scale cultural community that is now being restructured and downsized, like a white-collar workforce in corporate America. Or it may mean that artmaking will be like blue-collar American jobs—it will be shipped out to places where it can be done more economically: Marathon and Marfa, Texas; Virginia City and Tuscarora, Nevada; Jerome and Bisbee, Arizona, to name a few remote places where artists have been migrating. A curator at a Texas museum tells me, quite cheerfully, that artists will no longer live in New York, just come there periodically to deliver to the market, and I picture artists like campesinas come down from the hills with their burdens—but to a marketplace that is only a marketplace of objects, not of ideas. Artists in small towns could become the equivalents of *maquiladora* workers, making goods for an economy they cannot afford to participate in (and writers like me who depend on large libraries are in a tighter bind altogether). It may be that cities have, so to speak, raised their admission fees—by obliging those who wish to stay in San Francisco, for example, to join the dot-com economy. But paying that fee may mean abandoning the values and goals one came with, and the loss of those idealists and impractical characters will be a loss to the life of the city and the culture as a whole. Cities may keep their traditional

South of Market looking north, with Rigo's "Extinct" mural on the left, Charlie Chaplin coopted into an Apple Computer "Think Different" billboard in the center, and construction cranes on the right.

appearance while joining the suburbs and gated communities as places of predictability, homogeneity and political inertia. Those who can afford to make art in the center will come with their advantages in place, and though much good work may be produced, work critiquing and subverting the status quo may become rarer just as we need it most. Art won't die, but that old urban relationship between the poor, the subversive and the creative called bohemia will. For a long time, we have imagined that the death of cities will arise from the eradication of public space, but it may instead be the eradication of the affordable private space in which public life is incubated that will prove fatal.

The Last Barricades

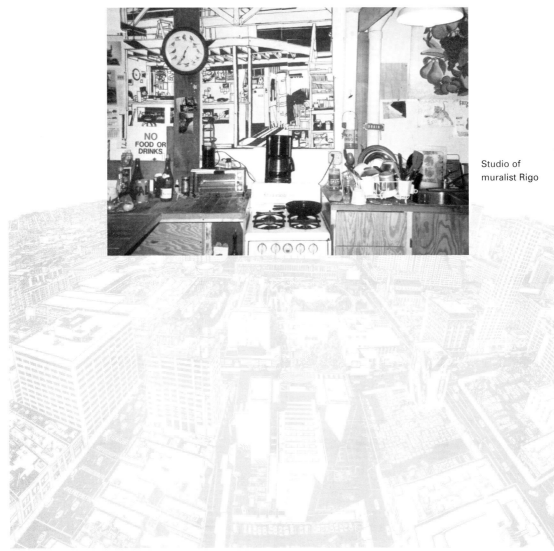

Studio of muralist Rigo

Rigo 1998, Study for Looking at 1998, San Francisco from 1925

Studio/home of an artist, woodworker, and musician who has lived here for 30 years. In June his landlord doubled his rent.

Studio of Debra Walker

Before I moved here, I did my work on the floor and stuck it under the bed when I was finished. The most important part of having a studio is that it's conducive. It's a kind of freedom—there is a certain space I go into when I'm working—like a trance. This is serious, and others may not understand. To be here, my work has gotten larger, my whole creative world has broadened.

This was one of the models of the live/work ordinance. We met with people from the City Planning Office about what we are. It's cheap here because we share facilities. There are bathrooms on each floor, and a kitchen. Some of us have stoves. I'm willing to trade off some of the comforts of "home" to be here. –*Debra Walker*

Cynthia Wallis at the kitchen computer station

I live here with Cynthia and my son. We work in the kitchen, or at this round table. When I moved to this place I had a separate studio, and then studio rents went up and up, and I lost the work space. I no longer have the luxury of going to a space and working on a large project. So the scale and scope of my work is a lot smaller. Lately as I go around the city, I take a razor blade with me and cut out fragments from posters, advertisements, trash, whatever I find, and bring them back and work with them.

My building is for sale, and people come through every day. I'm trying to buy it, but it's a half-million dollars. I may be forced to leave—you create community through performance and visual art. I am an urban artist. If I had to move to the suburbs, how would that effect my work?" –René Yanez

This profession is famous for not being able to make a living from it. But creative people always find a way. There are different kinds of artists, people who are part of a scene—and loners. But the moments when art, or "bohemian" situations thrive are temporary—difficult situations at best. Creativity thrives in the cracks, in decadence. That's often where culture grows, like bacteria in unhealthy dark areas, you see that throughout history, but they don't last. Where are we going to go now? That's what everyone asks. *–Emma Coleman and friend*

In 1998 my landlord called and said he was rethinking the economics of the building and evicted me. 'I'm an artist, too," he said. "I know how you feel." He'd already signed a lease with the guy downstairs, a web designer with a business called Concept Kitchen. I moved most of my work into storage, got a small office and began a nomadic art-life carting my work from space to space. I now work a lot out of a PowerBook in my studio apartment. Oddly, my work became more public—large-scale/permanent works, or books. I think a lot about storage and memory, and how easy it is to forget when chunks of your life are buried behind padlocks. –*S. Schwartzenberg*

Studio/home of Aaron Noble and Marisa Hernandez

A fear I'm considering as I face eviction is that I'll have to choose between living in the city and working as an artist. My work is urban, I'm urban. If cities become too expensive to live in, unless you work 40 hours a week or more—well, somehow I would continue. If I lose the studio I'll switch to painting miniatures, but I won't stop.

aron Noble entering his studio from Clarion alley through his
mural Super Hero Warehouse, a collaborative project with Rigo.

here are autonomous zones in the city, zones that nobody seems to care much about—vacant lots, undevel-
ped parcels, or even a disreputable alley, like this one. There is something about having these types of places
at are dead, and only relate to the past, that is somehow liberating, and in San Francisco there are so few
ft. There is some idea of balance in public terrain, and it's not just about danger—but places where there is
fe and stillness and adventure. *–Aaron Noble*

Opening night, San Francisco Opera, 1996.

Talking Dog, 1989. Drawing by Eric Drooker.

Skid Marks on the Social Contract

"Ah! So you would like to know why I hate you today?" opens Baudelaire's prose-poem "The Eyes of the Poor." The poem describes how the narrator and the feminine "you" of the piece sit down "in front of a new café forming the corner of a new boulevard still littered with rubbish but that already displayed proudly its unfinished splendors"—one of Haussmann's new boulevards cutting through the city. The café is ornamented with mirrors, gilding and classical figures, and the street delivers up a father with a tired face and his two ragged children who stare in at the luxurious scene: Paris is far from a gated community. "Not only was I touched by this family of eyes, but I was even a little ashamed of our glasses and decanters, too big for our thirst," continues the narrator, but his lover declares, "Those people are insufferable with their great saucer eyes. Can't you tell the proprietor to send them away?"[1] The piece is usually read as being about relations between classes, but the poor are just an occasion for exploring emotions within a class: "why I hate you today." The narrator and his lover are quite literally in the same position, with their seats and drinks, but they look out with different eyes.

In the debate over the fate of San Francisco and whose fault it is, there is a lot of hatred of a usually faceless "them" distinguished from "us." Among the distinctions made are those between old-timers and newcomers, those who don't work in high-tech and those who do, between bohemians and yuppies, or between a myriad of other distinctions: bicyclists versus those who own cars, tenants versus those who own homes, those who earn a certain amount more than the arbiter of the moment. Of course no hard line can be drawn: developers have been here all along, and starry-eyed idealists still arrive; some young artists and writers have found multimedia a useful source of freelance work that lets them continue their lives and art here; some artists make a lot of money selling art the old way; and after all, an MFA costs about the same amount as an MBA and is accessible to the same general group of people. Like the difference between the narrator and his lover, these differences are about attitude more than privilege. All that is certain is that a lot of people have recently arrived in San Francisco; many of them earn a lot and a few of them are spectacularly wealthy; their cumulative effect is transforming the city and the ability of many old-timers to stay in it; and the civility of the city is rapidly crumbling. I have written about the relations between those in the café of redevelopment and those who can only press up against its glass, but it's important to discuss another factor in this history, the differences of character and manners within the more or less middle class.

The crisis over housing literally gets people where they live, apartment by apartment, flat by flat. It's a largely invisible affair, except for the live/work condos gleaming amid the industrial districts. Live/work spaces, which aren't assessed school taxes, constitute a built-in negation of the social contract, but we have artists as well as developers to thank for that. Some of the nouveaux riches of San Francisco refuse to cohabit with the poor, the needy, the festive, and even with blue-collar work. (A recent arrival from Seattle who bought a loft condo in an industrial neighborhood complains that the Maritime Hall, a longtime nightclub nearby, "invites these people not just to the Maritime but to my neighborhood, where I pay a hell of a lot of money to live.")[2] As the Haight-Ashbury has become more affluent, tolerance has declined for social services and their clientele of drug users, homeless people and runaway kids. In the industrial neighborhoods, the buyers of live/work spaces are notorious for protesting and sometimes successfully shutting down the actual industries and cultural activities of the neighborhood. If true gentrification includes this kind of refusal to coexist, then bohemians are indeed a distinct and separate phenomenon, since they generally coexist enthusiastically. Too much affluence is not really good for urban culture: activism and the arts are dwindling, not multiplying, as affluence spreads here. This family quarrel is about the role of the rich in the decline of public life and about who to blame for the economic changes, which are not necessarily the same thing.

A city is a place where people have, as a rule, less private space and fewer private amenities because they share public goods—public parks, libraries, streets, cafés, plazas, schools, transit—and in the course of sharing them become part of a community, become citizens. In the ideal city, people regard the entire city as their home, so that the place they rent or own doesn't have to be fully equipped like a space capsule or a suburban home. Living in the city at large means coexisting with strangers, and not everyone seems to understand or value the social contracts by which one does so. Beyond the crisis over housing is the crisis over—manners? conduct? class?—which is evident across the nation, but particularly stark here, where the newly affluent arrived like an avalanche and public life had been among the nation's most vital. The *Noe Valley Voice,* one of a score of free community newspapers here, published an April Fool's Day issue whose teaser headlines read "Old Yuppies Decry New Yuppies" and "Pot Calls Kettle Black" and featured a spoof story on Rhoda Raige, widow of "former alcalde José de Jésus Noe," murdering the driver of a red "Behemoth PX4" who was "simultaneously talking on his cell phone and getting a pebble out of his shoe" while driving in this cushy neighborhood. A nearby photograph showed "a jovial crowd of computer haters, led by Ned Lud [sic], staged an April 1 candlelight march from Douglass Park to Radio Shack. The march broke up abruptly after a Palm Pilot fell out of a protester's rucksack and no one was able to stop it from beeping." The marchers in this spoof protest carried signs reading "URL go to Hell," "I'm P.O.'d at IPOs," and "Die, Dot Commies."[3] The humor was refreshing, but the feelings are real.

Civic life and cultural life everywhere are in decline because of the acceleration of work—both its acceleration and its takeover of more and more time. An increasing urgency governs everyday public acts—and the public sphere itself is more and more merely the space people pass through on errands and commutes. That sense of urgency breeds a harried selfishness far more threatening to public life in the cities of the new economy than, say, street crime. The accelerated and equipped use their cars and cell phones to dispel the safety, accessibility and civility of that space; they carry their private space with them, and privatization becomes not just an economic issue but a social attitude (expressed in such items as car alarms, which place the rights of private property in public over the auditory peace of the neighborhood). One could regard the privatized as victims of the high-pressure new economy, but participation in it at the level of, say, running a stop sign to get to work faster is likely to create more literal victims. San Francisco is being suburbanized by people who persist in driving everywhere, even though driving is a disastrous form of trans-

Together We Can Defeat Capitalism (artists' collective), mobile electronic message board, 2000. Courtesy New Langton Arts.

portation in this small, European-scale city: gridlock is common, parking is scarce in most parts of the city, and pedestrians were, in the first three months of 2000, being mowed down at the rate of almost one a week. Though San Francisco has the state's highest per capita pedestrian fatality rate, this may be in part because it still has pedestrians, those definitive figures of true urban life. Beleaguered pedestrians: walkers have largely surrendered their right of way and stand tentatively at curbs waiting to see if approaching cars will really stop at the stop sign or the red light; if they cross at a crosswalk at which a car is waiting, they scuttle deferentially. Only the daring and defiant bicycle. The sense of the city as home is eroding as the public sphere ceases to be a place where people feel at home; the infrastructure has remained charming and compact, but the new arrivals seem to live in it as though it were a suburb. One has the sense that San Francisco—which used to be nicknamed "the city that knows how"—is populated by people who just don't get urbanism or just don't value it.

Urban life, like cultural life, requires a certain leisure, a certain relaxation, a certain willingness to engage with the unknown and unpredictable. For those who feel impelled to accelerate, the unknown and the unpredictable are interference as the city's public space becomes not a place to *be* but a place to traverse as rapidly as possible. The social darwinism that has been the prevailing social policy since Reagan took office has, among other things, led to an every-man-for-himself anti-etiquette at odds with the countless small acts of cooperation that make a city functional and livable. In parks, on buses, the ring of cell phones and the projective voices of those chatting on them means that everyone in the vicinity is forced to take up auditory residence in the speaker's virtual office or home (while pay phones, which created comparatively democratic and semi-secluded sites for such conversation, are vanishing). Like bad drivers, loud cell-phone users suggest the unimportance of the here they share

Together We Can Defeat Capitalism (artists' collective), mobile electronic message board, 2000. Courtesy New Langton Arts.

South of Market billboard, 2000.

with strangers in comparison with the now-virtual there of work and private life. The new technology is geared toward convenience—insofar as participating in the public sphere, traveling, moving, watching and waiting, and encountering the unknown face-to-face are conceptualized as inconvenient and inefficient. Such technology may not be responsible for but it is certainly accommodating spatial privatization and speeding up an economic privatization. It postulates the public sphere as a problem to which technology is the solution, whether it saves one from venturing out to buy books or groceries or from asking directions from a stranger. There is a real sense in San Francisco that the social contract is being torn up by those who own it. The social contract has been steadily dismantled over the past two decades by the elimination of social services, by the creation of a two-tier economy, by the creation of a homeless population many Americans are too young or too forgetful to remember hardly existed two decades ago. But I don't believe the changes in public life are about clear-cut difference in economic status, but differences in values and priorities. I'm with the narrator of "The Eyes of the Poor"; I can now afford nice drinks but I am unsure about an economy and a spatial divide that shuts out the poor and denies our obligations and connections to each other. I am also unsure whether we can neatly define louts as a socioeconomic category and whether hate is a useful response.

Kevin Keating *is* sure about it, and like the narrator of "The Eyes of the Poor," his revelation came in a café. Keating is the founder and principal of the Mission Yuppie Eradication Project, which has thus far consisted of three series of posters put up in that neighborhood in 1998, 1999 and after our interview in 2000. I met Keating in the Café Picaro one evening, and he told me, "It wasn't like there was one Road to Damascus–type of event but there was one thing that sticks out in my mind. I'm sitting in my favorite café, the Atlas Café, at the corner of Alabama and 20th, and the next table over there's this guy. He's got a laptop open on the table in front. The laptop is turned on. He's talking very animatedly with this kind of bovine hubris on his cell phone to some guy he keeps referring to as 'jeffster, dude' and I'm looking at this dot-com alien over at this next table and wondering what he's doing here."[5] A thin man with thinning brown hair, Keating talks rapidly, with key phrases that surface again and again in his vocabulary combining Marxist phrases and post-adolescent slurs. He had asked me to meet him in the Café Picaro, which was one of the first cafés in the Mission District and is now really a tapas restaurant. I remember it long ago in what must have been the mid-1980s, when it had walls of books, served mostly lattes and bagels. A sinewy old wacko with tattered clothes and his face painted red under a big sombrero used to drift through it. As Keating, who moved to San Francisco a dozen years ago, put it, "It used to be this was the great café of the Mission back in the 1980s and then Carlos the guy who owns it thought he'd make it yuppie-oriented by putting Almodóvar posters and melting clocks on the wall." Still, Keating had chosen it as our rendezvous spot because he said it had "great *vino rojo*," and when he found out the drinks were on me, he ordered a second and a third and then a fourth glass of it.

Keatings's Mission Yuppie Eradication Project, which may or may not have included others, had put up a poster proposing that locals vandalize expensive cars in the neighborhood:

Over the past several years the Mission has been colonized
by pigs with money. Yuppie scumbags have crawled out of
their haunts on Union Street and the suburbs to take our neighborhood
away from us. They go to restaurants like The Slanted Door and
Ti-Couz and bars like Skylark and Liquid. They come to party, and
end up moving into what used to be affordable rental housing. They
help landlords drive up rents, pushing working and poor people
out of their homes.

Now Buffy and Chip are moving into "lawyer lofts" built
by real estate speculators in the Mission's northeast corner,
further gutting our neighborhood.

This yuppie takeover can be turned back.
We can drive these cigar bar clowns back to Orinda
and Walnut Creek where they belong.

VANDALIZE YUPPIE CARS
BMWs - Porsches - Jaguars
SPORT UTILITY VEHICLES

• Break the Glass
• Scratch the Paint
• Slash Their Tires and Upholstery
• Trash Them All

"The first ones were only in English. The second ones were in English and Spanish. They're titled *Soon to Be Picturesque Ruins* —from Paris, the Situationists spraypainted it on the walls of the Bourse, the Stock Exchange, you know 'this building is soon to be in picturesque ruins....' They [the posters] suggested that in the major urban riots, you must attack and destroy the following yuppie bars and restaurants in the Mission: the

Beauty Bar; the Tokyo A-Go-Go, this yuppie restaurant up the street; Blowfish Sushi; and Circadia—Circadia's like a closet Starbucks on the corner of Mariposa and Bryant." As an aside, he explained, "I don't hate sushi, I love sushi, you know, I just hate certain yuppie sushi restaurants that are this colonization of the Mission District." Keating goes on to ruminate, "It's funny to think that there's been only two posters. All that media attention and there were only two posters. The first one … explains in jargon-free terms what gentrification is. Not to blow my own horn or anything, but I think it really succeeded as revolutionary propaganda because its message was completely transparent without saying anything about capitalism or bourgeois society or proletariats or Marx. They communicate the message and anybody who knew what side of the class divide on which they fell—now that's not to say that all working people, all wage-slaves, identify with what was on the posters, I mean who fetishizes the private automobile more than the working class? One of the other good things is that the posters had these wide margins. I didn't set it up that way…." The margins, he explained, allowed people to write commentary on the posters. "Somebody wrote, 'Ignore this poster, I know the guy who puts this up, he's a fucking yuppie himself,' which I'm not.

"I'm basically this urban bohemian déclassé type. You know, I never wanted to have a career, a job that was going to tell me what to do with my life. I never wanted to become a professional intellectual or an academic or anything like that. I did go to school but I just studied things that were of interest to me and used school basically as a way of avoiding wage labor and made my first 16-millimeter film and learned how to write fiction. And I always really loved San Francisco. It sounds really sappy, but I always thought San Francisco was the most romantic city in all of North America, one of the only cities of really unique character in the English-speaking world. Unfortunately, people like me who want to get as far away from the mainstream as we can without actually leaving the United States altogether end up gravitating to neighborhoods like Manhattan's Lower East Side, Alphabet City, and San Francisco's Mission District and then we end up initiating the whole process of gentrification...."

Keating, who is going on forty, struck me mostly as an anachronism. A mailroom clerk in an architectural firm—which was, he admitted, participating in altering the city too—he had based his life on the promise that a white kid could work a job his heart wasn't in, mess around with the arts, espouse a little revolutionary rhetoric and appreciate the ambience without feeling too much pressure. The new economy, however, had voided that slacker warranty of the 1980s. And his fantasies of mass uprising seemed more anachronistic yet, like something out of the sixties, when white kids thought they were going to spark the revolution rather than, say, laboriously organize social change or serve in someone else's revolution; while his distinctions between good and evil sushi bars seemed a little subtle. Finally, can a deteriorating public life and declining public manners be fought with threats and insults? Still, Keating cannot be merely dismissed: his posters stirred up a debate, and nobody was then doing better posters about the subject. And he cares about his neighborhood. Some actual vandalism has taken place—the Beauty Bar was graffitied—but mostly the Yuppie Eradication posters served as a prank or, à la Greenpeace, a media stunt in which the act itself was immensely magnified by its reproduction in newspapers everywhere. Keating got great international coverage and was actually arrested, had his house searched, and a lot of his property was confiscated. "I couldn't work on my novel, I was trying to write the great American novel for years and years and years, and my attorney and I went to court ten or twelve times to get them to give me back my stuff"—but the ruckus has died down now. Mostly it was a 1998 phenomenon, and there was a more important surge of activism in 1999.

The heated mayoral runoff race in late 1999 between incumbent Mayor Willie Brown and insurgent candidate Tom Ammiano was a war of sorts about what kind of a city San Francisco should be, and for whom. It was a surprise to everyone, including Ammiano and Brown. Ammiano, a gay man who used to teach grade school before going into politics, is a meekly principled figure, a sort of Mr. Rogers of radical politics, a tenants' rights advocate, a public transit rider, and one of the few members of the Board of Supervisors Brown didn't appoint. After declining to run despite the urging of supporters, Ammiano jumped in as a write-in candidate six weeks before the November election and galvanized city politics for a brief movement. Josie's Juice Joint and Cabaret, a gay performance spot in the Castro (since closed), became campaign headquarters, and thousands of volunteers streamed in to precinct-walk, phone-bank, poster, fundraise and generally take a last stab at hanging onto their city. Ammiano's candidacy gave those volunteers a hope and a means that had been sadly lacking in the juggernaut of the Brown-administered San Francisco. Brown himself had once been the radical outsider, an African-American candidate in the days when that in itself was radical, and a civil rights and free-speech activist, but during his decades in the state capital he became a human incarnation of political machinery, famous for his expensive clothes and cars, cronyism, vengefulness, coercive tactics and ties to developers. He is a twenty-first-century Boss Tweed, or perhaps he's just Clintonian neoliberalism, which believes in human rights only when they don't interfere with the free market.

Another way to view the changes wracking San Francisco now is as the end of an era even briefer than that of postwar prosperity. In the 1970s another culture clash took place, between conservative longtime San Franciscans and the ascendant gay and progressive communities—the reactionary Dan White's 1978 assassination of fellow supervisor Harvey

Together We Can Defeat Capitalism (artists' collective), mobile electronic message board, 2000. Courtesy New Langton Arts.

Milk and Mayor George Moscone was part of that clash. Now, as a recent *San Francisco Chronicle* essay noted, those who won the battle of the 1970s—progressives, bohemians—are losing the battle of the 1990s. Ammiano seemed to represent the ascendant 1970s communities, but the actual gay community was divided.[6] Some of the gay Democratic clubs had already endorsed Brown, and some gay businessmen found Ammiano's ideas about housing, transit, taxes and development too radical. Most of Ammiano's support came from the neighborhoods that give San Francisco its identity—the denser central districts, where diversity and public life most flourish. In the general election, he came in second out of a field of five, despite being the latecoming lowest spender. By the time Brown won the runoff—by a percentage in the high teens—he had spent $5 million to win the race and drawn support from big business, developers and out-of-town interests, including the statewide Democratic Party machine he had helped to build. Wrote the *Chronicle*'s political columnists, "Never has a San Francisco politician had such a barrage of 'soft money' support as Willie Brown in the final days of this election." Someone spray-stenciled on my corner and many others, "People who make less than $50,000 don't belong here—Willie Brown," a spurious but genuine-sounding quote from a mayor who famously did say, "Democracy is best served by my running unopposed." Read one popular campaign button, "Another terrified tenant for Tom." Ammiano's sponsors included the San Francisco Tenants Union, the Bicycle Coalition and thousands of volunteers. It was a last-ditch effort to save the old San Francisco, by and for the people who constituted its key population.

While I was writing this chapter, Supervisor Amos Brown evicted an elderly tenant who is, fittingly enough, named Love, along with her gay son, who has cerebral palsy, and infant grandson. Amos Brown, who was appointed by Willie Brown (no relation), is an African-American minister who has been more hostile to the homeless than any other elected official and who is calling for a study of rent control that is widely suspected to be the first step in dismantling tenant-protection laws. The eviction of Edith Love from the modest Ingleside house Brown owned allegedly took place so that he could run for election in that district rather than against powerful Supervisor Mabel Teng, who lives in the (wealthier) district where Brown currently resides. With help from a homeless organization she contacted, Love found a new place to live, despite Brown's refusal to return her deposit and other acts that made the eviction far crueler than necessary. She later went public to say that she was not happy with the poorer neighborhood she had moved to, in part because the new neighbors made homophobic remarks to her son, and that the reverend had pressured her to say she had moved voluntarily rather than was evicted.[8] Meanwhile, Supervisor Leslie Katz—another Brown appointee who had got a lucrative job at Pets.com—is proposing an end run around Proposition M, the 1986 slow-growth initiative that limits new office space to a hardly sparse 950,000 square feet a year. In Katz's proposal, there would be no limits whatsoever on Internet companies—and therefore on the housing crisis they're creating. (The campaign to exempt multimedia offices from office-space limits is another attempt to evade paying social dues, similar to the aggressive national campaign to prevent Internet commerce from paying any tax at all and is one of the ways the Internet undermines the public sphere. (Bookstores, for example, function as part of communities, both as gathering places and as local taxpayers, and they are being undermined by online bookstore goliaths.) Leslie Katz and Amos Brown, lesbian and African American, exemplify the difficulty of categorizing the players in this new shakeup. The category, as Baudelaire's "Eyes of the Poor" makes clear, is not as clearcut as race or class or orientation; it is a moral category defined by opportunism and lack of empathy.

One thing worth keeping in mind is that landlords in San Francisco were for the most part making a tidy profit before the tsunani.com hit in 1997, and certainly none of them seemed to be going bust. San Francisco's epidemic of evictions, the Weimar-style inflation in housing prices, the malicious harassment of tenants—often of elderly and ill tenants—is all taking place so that people who are making a profit can make a bigger profit, even an obscene profit. Thus are they purging the aptly named nonprofits of the city: in a recent poll, 70 percent of the nonprofits had leases that expired in 36 months, 50 percent in a year, and since almost all of them are facing unaffordable rent increases of up to 600 percent, greed is creating a mass exodus of the organizations that make this a livable and a visionary city. Since residential tenants are largely protected, the tactics are more roundabout. One woman—a splendid community-minded activist who may not be here much longer—mentioned that among her landlord's tactics to drive her out was to come and chainsaw all her old-growth cacti (which were legally his, since it was his land). The man she was speaking to responded with a tale of a landlord's rosebush massacre: apparently even herbicide has entered the strategic arsenal. In this light, the arriving dot-commies are just the settlers moving into the cleared land, not the cavalry clearing it.

Some of the more thoughtful, outraged and progressive people I've met work for dot-coms; two of the most vile landlords I've heard about have fair local reputations as artists; there are no clear lines to be drawn in the high-speed spin of change. I heard about one guy who planned to drop out of the Internet economy as soon as he had made enough to set himself up in an otherwise impoverishing career as a schoolteacher, and I heard a caller on a local radio show say that he couldn't quit his six-figure tech job because he wanted to stay where his family has lived for generations. Another reason the difference between "us" and "them" is so difficult to ascertain is that people change sides. Carol Lloyd, a writer who now works for the online magazine *Salon* and owns a flat in the Mission District, wrote there in the fall of 1999 that "As a dyed-in-the-wool progressive, community-volunteering, social-working artist, I was once a member of the endangered species that these activists are so diligently trying to save from extinction. What happened? I got a job—in the scurrilously libertarian Internet sector —that allowed me to buy a home. That alone has transported me across the battle lines. The problem is that in San Francisco downward mobility had become a lifestyle choice every bit as self-indulgent as upward mobility. I know because I was one of the voluntarily low-income: lionizing the working class, despising my 'white-skinned' privilege, camouflaging the capriciousness of my aesthetic tastes, nursing a love-hate relationship with the middle-class identity my parents imbued in me. There is a real pleasure and even, I think, a virtue in that kind of voluntary poverty, but it really doesn't have much in common with the poverty in my neighborhood."[9]

It's easy to see Lloyd and Keating as the discordant lovers in Baudelaire's café. In the poem's terms, she hates him because he hates her, and he hates her because she disdains those left out by the gentrifying city. Lloyd makes some important points—for example, that a lot of children of the middle class are in a muddle about their social roles, and that for immigrant families, the Mission District is not necessarily romantic (Dick Walker points out that the Mission's Latino population surged during Central America's dirty wars of the 1980s and is dropping in part because many of them are heading for more affluent neighborhoods and burbs). But Lloyd is on the defensive, in part because the argument is being conducted on Keatings' terms as an indictment of the empowered. It's a problem that speaks to a pervasive political stance in left-of-center culture: that if power corrupts and abuses, then the virtuous are not necessarily those who fight the power, but those who claim not to have any: the triumph of the victim. Lloyd's defensiveness is betrayed by some of her more specious points: she uses an African-American dot-com guy as evidence that the changes in the Mission aren't racial (and in a similar piece written in May 2000, uses a twice-evicted Latino artist who just joined a dot-com to similarly murky purpose). And she misses the most important point: that the realm she left behind is genuinely imperiled, and that it has real value. Even if it includes some of the most annoying and silly people you could meet, this realm also harbors muralists, tenant organizers, teachers, environmentalists, experimentalists, human rights advocates. The downwardly mobile create a wide-open social space that the upwardly mobile, whatever their color, are helping to eliminate. That space is a laboratory for the young to experiment with their identities, a laboratory many voluntarily leave later for more conventional lives and smaller towns, taking something of their transformation with them. Others emerge out of it to succeed as artists or become more traditional activists, with salaries and offices. There is no way to regulate this bohemian space and no reason to regulate it so that only the talented and the dedicated can enter. The civility of public life is a far slipperier thing, hard to preserve except by example, and infinitely vulnerable to being run over, shouted down or shoved aside. On the other hand, though upscale consumers with bad manners are undermining public life and public space in many parts of the city, when it comes to the feverish changes brought by the new economy they're not the viral agents, just the itchy spots.

"Come Enjoy the Mission," an anonymous poster plastered across the Mission District in September 2000. This example on the window of what was once the live-music center Radio Valencia overlays NASDAQ Index pages from the business section. Around the corner paintbombs splashed the Bayview Bank Building, where Bigstep.com displaced several Latino service organizations.

Hunters Point Restaurant, a 1940s-era diner built to serve workers at the Hunters Point Shipyard. After the shipyard closed, it became a neighborhood club. It closed recently to make room for the new development along the city's southern waterfront.

Amnesia Is a Club

"I started to feel like a stranger in my own neighborhood, I started to feel like I didn't have that much holding me there," says the graphic artist Nick Kozloff, who was a dedicated anti-gentrification artist in the Lower East Side during the late 1980s. His street posters dealt with, in his words, "real estate, landlord terrorism, police brutality." Allen Ginsberg, who also lived in the Lower East Side, was a fan who collected Kozloff's posters off the street, and the two did a book together; Kozloff has also done *New Yorker* covers and graphics for numerous progressive causes. Two years ago, after a lifetime on the east side of Manhattan, he moved to Haight Street in San Francisco. One afternoon I went to visit and from his drawing board in the small room that is also his bedroom he told me, "People ask me out here, 'Nick, don't you ever feel homesick for New York?' And I say, 'Yes, sometimes I do, but I've been feeling homesick for years.' In New York I was feeling homesick the last five or ten years. I felt like I had the carpet pulled out from under me, things changed so much. It was pretty dramatic after staying in one place my whole life. You stay in one place and watch everything change around you. You definitely don't notice it unless you've been in the same place for five, ten years, if not twenty or thirty years, and then you really get perspective. I love New York but I felt four decades was a long stretch. I know exactly what people are talking about [with gentrification here], but I don't really see it because I just got here. New York is so painful to me when I go back and see that things from my childhood are no longer there. It's unrecognizable. Here the same destruction is going on, but I don't perceive it because I have nothing to compare it to. It looks good to me."

It doesn't look so good to those who have been here longer. There must be a rate at which one forgets, and as long as a city changes at that rate or a slower one, change registers but it doesn't disorient, for there are sufficient points of orientation and triggers of recollection. For those who spend years in a place, their own autobiography becomes embedded in it so that the place becomes a text they can read to remember themselves, to muse, as well as a collection of landmarks of minor and major historical events. Every city changes, and walking through a slowly changing city is like walking through an organic landscape during various seasons; leaves and even trees fall, birds migrate, but the forest stands: familiarity anchors the changes. But if the pace of change accelerates, a disjuncture between memory and actuality arises and one moves through a city of phantoms, of the disappeared, a city that is lonely and disorienting; one becomes, like Kozloff, an exile at home. The urban forest can be clear-cut and defoliated. To have your city dismantled too rapidly around you is to have the relationship between mind and place thrown into disarray, to have it stripped of meaning, silenced, and this is part of what disturbed the Parisian writers and strollers during Haussmann's redevelopment. Visual art is a material medium, but at its best it makes the material a vessel to be filled with stories, ideas, desires, subversions, provocations. It invests matter with life, and history does something similar to cities: it makes buildings, streets, squares and parks come to life and voice. In a place with a rich culture and cultural memory, an interchange is forever taking place between mind and material. When culture and memory are evicted from a city, its places, its locations and its products become mute commodities that can be purchased but not dreamed.

While I have been writing this book, I have been watching my local grocery, Falletti's Foods, be reduced to piles of rubble and rebar. My neighborhood had the last of the great Italian ur-supermarkets that once spread across the city. A nonchain union grocery with particularly good produce, separate shops selling meat, fish, poultry, baked goods, and wine, along with a pharmacy and a delicatessen, it was a sort of Europeanate market under one pink stucco roof. The place opened in 1956 and had been part of the neighborhood ever since: it stocked soul food as well as gourmet products, and the checkers and managers knew lots of customers by name. It closed with the twentieth century. The land underneath it was sold to a developer, and a huge Lucky supermarket complex with 130 market-rate condos was slated for the site, though Albertson's acquired Lucky's before ground was broken. For the first few months of 2000, I had to check the almost physical reflex to go out for an ingredient at the last minute. The abandoned site was surrounded with chain-link fence and a lot of local taggers came and graffitied it. One particularly ornate piece on the back wall said "Future 2000," and I read that as an editorial. Then came the wreckers, and day by day the site that corresponded to my fresh memory of the store was dismantled into heaps of concrete, rebar and I-beams. I went away for a few days and when I came back, even the "Future 2000" wall was gone. The store now exists only in memory, though there I can still go straight to the brown sugar or the basil. The vista the demolition opened up is exhilarating, but vacant lots everywhere are being filled in, and this one will be built up far more than the Falletti site ever was.

Of course, what one remembers is not necessarily primordial, and all cities sit atop erased landscapes. When City Lights Books, as hallowed a San Francisco institution as they come, was being seismically upgraded, an actual stream was uncovered, still flowing beneath the basement. Like the sand that shows up every time a building is demolished to remind us that San Francisco was once mostly just dunes, the rivulet that runs through City Lights is a reminder that North Beach covers a lost landscape. Once an old man stopped me on Chestnut Street in North Beach to point out where there had been a soap factory facing the water, before landfill took the beachfront further north. His story enlarged the way I can imagine this place I often pass through, gave me one more ghost of the past with which to populate it.

I have lived in one place long enough to watch it go from a neighborhood with no trees and lots of parking to the reverse as it evolved from a poor, predominantly African-American neighborhood full of people who saluted each other by name on the street to one that was for a long time a stable mixed community and that has, in the past few years, suddenly gentrified and clogged with SUVs parked on the sidewalks where children used to jump rope and women walk to church—SUVs belonging to people who are seldom seen. You have to stand still to witness the movement of populations, economics, cities. Because I grew up nearby, I can just barely remember Playland at the Beach, the amusement park destroyed in the late 1960s that had been cited as an inspiration by the artist Jess and was paid homage to more recently by the artist Ray Beldner, who grew up visiting it regularly. I can remember the mid-1980s vacant lot at 16th and Valencia and its graffiti about landlord arson but I can't remember the building that was there before, though Susan Schwartzenberg can. I have been arguing with a friend about whether the club on

Valencia Street called Amnesia used to be the Club Chameleon, but I can readily remember the ancient pharmacy on Haight Street that went out of business a year or so ago. In its windows were huge prescription books from early in the twentieth century, and the careful copperplate handwriting, the drugs prescribed and the ethnicity of the names listed spoke of a civilization entirely different from that inhabited by the current swarms of adolescents and plethora of stores selling platform shoes. The pharmacy window thus became a window into history, a recollection of a Haight district few alive remembered.

Many of the nonchain businesses in the city—upholstery shops, hardware stores—display photographs of the business or the neighborhood long ago. This is one of the incalculable benefits of these nonchains: they sell commodities but they give out history, memory, a sense of place, local flavor, community knowledge. Across the street from the destroyed Italian foodstore, a donut shop became a burrito shop in the 1980s that went from being a great place to a sad one, and then it suddenly became a Starbucks, and to step inside a Starbucks is to step from the particular to the generic, from memorable location to the limbo of the chain that makes Philadelphia, Seattle and Albuquerque indistinguishable. Cities were born free but are everywhere in chains, and these chains erase the particulars by which we know a city and the noncommodity goods we get from the places we frequent: they chain our minds to mere commodities. Like the mass-manufactured goods that introduced one kind of alienation in the Industrial Revolution, corporate chains introduce another in this era of global capital, an alienation from geography, from place. Chains such as Starbucks are scariest of all, because they impersonate the sensibility of nonchains, while McDonald's is at least honest about its mass-production values. There are sixty Starbucks in San Francisco now, and to step into any one of them is to enter limbo, albeit limbo with good graphic design.

Memory is being removed from San Francisco with the rubble of old buildings, the demise of nonchain businesses, the outmigration of economically uncompetitive people and the arrival of newcomers who live in a city as though it were a suburb. Memory is being evicted. I think we move forward as rowers do, facing the receding shore of the past, and memory provides the landmarks ashore that let us navigate a coherent path. The commemoration of the past becomes a path into the future, just as parades and processions are commemorations of past events that let participants lay claim to present power or the creation of a future. From Art and Revolution's pageant at the conclusion of last year's May Day Parade to Dolores Park, I know that Emma Goldman once lived in a house facing its green slopes, and that she and Alexander Berkman briefly published *Blast* there. It took a parade that is a commemoration of workers' history and a celebration of the presence of radicals now to give me that small nugget of local history, and at the February 2000 youth rally opposing another draconian prison measure for minors, I realized that the youths were rapping in front of Emma's house, so that two histories of resistance suddenly aligned and moved me to tears. Walking down Harrison Street south of Market the other night, I passed doorways with homeless people sleeping in them, as brightly illuminated as though they were in window displays, and then an expensive, dimly lit restaurant and then, across the street, a high-rise building whose tile-mosaic entryway floor I saw for the first time. It said Mendelsohn, and I realized that this was Mendelsohn House, named after one of the elderly residential hotel tenants who had fought Yerba Buena redevelopment so valiantly. The sequence— homeless / upscale / commemoration at the entry of a residence that had saved at least some vulnerable citizens from homelessness—made a narrative, and thanks to Ira Nowinski's photographs I could read it. Nick Kozloff was a repository of stories even after the subjects of some of his stories, human and architectural, had been displaced, but now he is like a book that has checked itself out of the library of New York stories; his memory is no longer facing his community. To lose the people who know a city, to lose a lot of them quickly, is like burning its library.

Of course we did burn our library in San Francisco, more or less. The 1989 Loma Prieta earthquake severely damaged the Main Library, pushing forward the long-held plan for a new library. The 1917 Beaux Arts build-ing had in any case been too small for the collection for decades. But sev-eral surprising things happened under the direction of chief librarian Ken Dowlin. The new library, built at a cost of about $130 million, actually contained fewer linear feet of shelf space than the old, though the new building was far larger. Its space was taken up with a cafe, a gift shop, a lot of computer terminals and a lot of open space; Dowlin was a techno-phile who occasionally suggested that books were going to become obsolete anyway. No foxier bureaucrat has ever guarded a henhouse, for the shortage

San Francisco's old Main Library being gutted in early 2000 before redevelop-ment as the new Asian Art Museum.

of shelf space was only the beginning of the story. The library had a huge purge of books, and thousands of old and not-so-old books ended up in a landfill before public outcry bent the rule that prohibited selling or donat-ing books. Though the official story was that the books were damaged, outdated or redundant, I found that several excellent and distinctive books I had been using in the old library had disappeared from the shelves and the records of the new, which opened in 1996. "First and foremost, SFPL is a public library, not a research facility," Dowlin wrote in defense of his position that the general public needed only the most popular works and that dumping old and obscure books was legitimate librarianship.[2]

Valencia Street storefront awaiting redevelopment.

The novelist Nicholson Baker and the historian Gray Brechin led the countercharge. Baker, who had moved from New York to Berkeley and already written a landmark essay about what was lost when card catalogues were discarded, sneaked into the old library and measured its shelf space. He came up with a figure approximately twice that of Dowlin's to buttress his charge that the new library did not even fulfill its primary purpose of increasing shelf space (much of the collection has ever since languished in closed stacks and underground storage). Brechin and Baker spoke out publicly and organized, and Baker even filed a lawsuit to access the old card catalogue (which, when the heat was high, was supposed to be part of the new library but was also shuffled off into inaccessible storage). Brechin wrote incendiary letters to the editor charging that "contrary to what was promised, the new Main has less room for books than the old building did. To accommodate what little it does hold, Ken Dowlin, the head librarian, progressively ordered his staff to dispose of up to a fifth of the existing collection, much of which was sent to a dump and buried. Most of the remaining collection is now in underground storage under unsafe conditions. Rather than storing knowledge, the building appeared to be designed for parties for the corporate and individual donors whose names so garishly adorn the central mall and the boutiques off of it. This is a public building mostly paid for by the citizens; it is not Planet Hollywood. The people of San Francisco, and a grand jury, need to ask why the city has a librarian whose enthusiasm for high technology appears to have led him to an active hatred of printed material...."[3] When the library scandals erupted, Brechin had already moved from San Francisco to Berkeley; Baker has since moved from Berkeley to Maine. What will happen to such public places and public institutions when the people who understand their value and have the time and the voice to fight for them aren't within reach? Voices with nothing to speak of and places with no one to speak for them?

If I had an acre for every person who has told me I can live anywhere because it's all on the Internet, I could abandon writing and set up as a cattle baroness. Iain Boal, a professor in UC Berkeley's Geography Department, has described the Internet as a vehicle of organized forgetting of the past before 1993. Scattered tidbits of the past are available on this medium, but most of its information is commercial and contemporary. It will never replace libraries and archives, and for a writer such as myself its primary research use is to access online archives of print media (by which means I have done a good deal of the research for this book, though other books of mine have taxed the resources of UC Berkeley's vast libraries and archives). In pursuit of the history of the San Francisco Public Library via Internet, I was stymied by the fact that the *San Francisco Chron-*

icle's online archives go back only to 1995, and the *San Francisco Bay Guardian*'s archives "temporarily" go back only six months. The only way I can retrace the library scandals of 1994 is to hunt down the participants or search for microfilm in a library, and these are local tasks. I remember the last Sunday I went to the library to look something up before I went online: I went to the farmers' market next door, bought produce, ran into a friend, witnessed a few minor dramas, talked to a homeless person and found my material. Researching on the Internet is a little like going to a chain store; I won't come home with pomegranates, and there seems to be a link between the textureless, amnesiac information the Internet most often brings us as it encourages not to go outside and the loss of urban texture and memory.

Movie billboard with full-color Spanish-language posters informing tenants of their rights and contact organizations, Mission District, 2000.

When the Gold Rush came to California, a horde of newcomers came in, and a lot of them didn't plan to stay any longer than it took to get rich. The Mexican-American locals whose history went back several decades here were displaced and often dispossessed, and the Native Americans of the Motherlode were massacred, starved and driven out. A huge chunk of history was lost with the memories of those victims of the boom, and the first versions of San Francisco were lost because they were built in a hurry and had a habit of burning down. Susan Miller of New

Langton Arts on Folsom Street says, "Being South of Market is like being at ground zero. I just watch it change every day. I can walk out the door every day and say 'Huh, I didn't notice that before....' The wealth that we're experiencing here and why it seems like a shock, like an earthquake, is because it's happening all at once and it's broad-based.... One of the big changes is architecture—how people thought differently about architecture.... The sense of quality and craft has changed; things tend to be done a little more on the cheap, and the culture that's being brought in with this money is about short-term gain: keep your job for two years, get all your stock options, your millions, and you're out doing something else and businesses are thinking that way. I was just talking to a dot-com owner just down the street from us and he was saying, 'Yeah, we're all just building it so that it can go away in a second.'"[4]

492 geary 2000p
275 o'farrell 2000p
1231 market 1997
1455 market 2000p (pasqua)
901 market 2000p (pasqua)
395 sutter
780 market 1999
1298 howard 2000p
101 4th 2000
120 4th 2000
226 kearny 2000p (pasqua)
264 kearny 1996
555 california 2000p (pasqua)
44 mongomery 2000p (pasqua)
730 howard 2000? (pasqua)
74 n. montgom 1996
36 2nd st) - 2000 p
369 pine 1995
15 sutter 2000p (pasqua)
2018 church ?
565 clay 2000p (pasqua)
343 sansome 1994
200 pine 2000p (pasqua)
505 sansome 1998
123 battery 1997
455 market 2000
398 market 2000? (pasqua)

303 sacramento 2000p (p
333 market 2000p (pasqua)
701 battery 2000 p
50 beale 2000p (pasq
340 market 2000p
27 drumm 2000
52 california 2000p
99 jackson 1996
123 mission 1999
1725 battery 2010 p
1 market 2000p
201 spear 1996
2 harrison 2000p (pasqua)

San Francisco in Chains
a project by Kate Joyce

We supplied stuff people needed and they would
come from all over. Then the neighborhood started
to change. First it was Fox Photo, then Copy Mat,
Le Petite Boulangerie; more and more chains all the
time. It brought on a whole change in retailing and
we just lost the business.

— *Former business owner on Union Street*

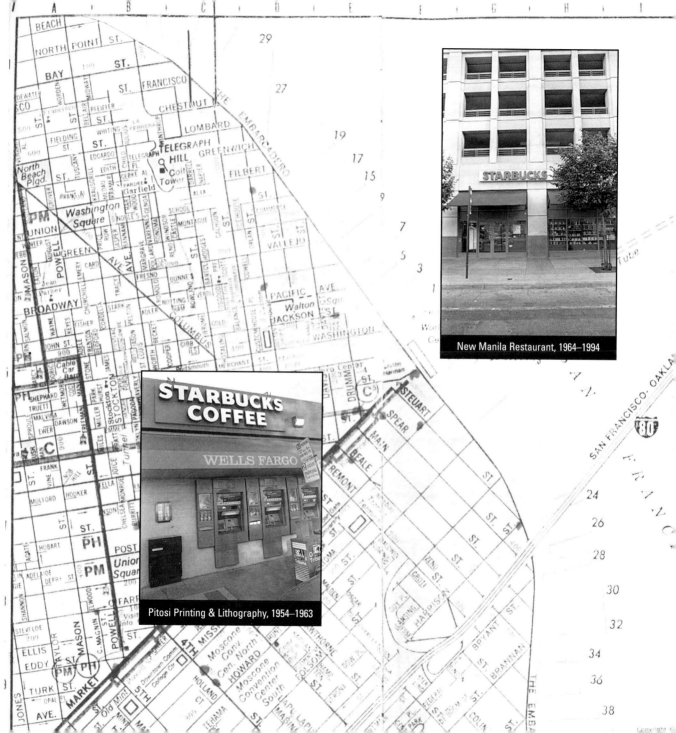

New Manila Restaurant, 1964–1994

Pitosi Printing & Lithography, 1954–1963

Circus Doughnuts, 1961–1985

The Captain's Scribe (card store), 1983–199

Ratto Hardware 1934-1992

Jeff's Jeans, 1978–1999

Duo Restaurant, 1978–1995

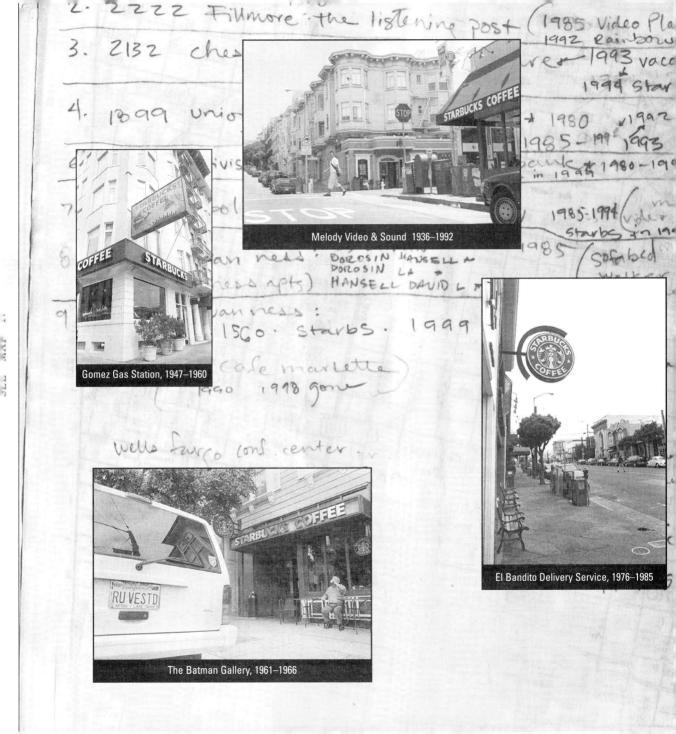

2. 2222 Fillmore - the listening post (1985 Video Pla
3. 2132 ches   1992 Rainbow
                                                          re — 1993 vaco
4. 1899 unio   1999 Star

                                                   * 1980   1992
                                                   1985 - 199   1993
                                              ivis   ink * 1980 - 199
                                                                in 1999
                                              ol
                                                                1985 - 1994 (vdeo
                                                                starbs in 19
                                                          985   Sofatbed
an ness   DOROSIN HANSELL   Walk
ess apts)   DOROSIN LA
            HANSELL DAVID L
an ness :
    1560 · starbs · 1999
    (afe marlette)
    go   1998 gone

wells fargo conf. center ..

Melody Video & Sound 1936–1992

Gomez Gas Station, 1947–1960

El Bandito Delivery Service, 1976–1985

The Batman Gallery, 1961–1966

Delivered Vacant

René Yanez is interviewing a burrito. "Why so angry, burrito?" he almost croons in a deep voice, holding a microphone to the big white food log atop a pedestal. "I'm getting evicted," says the voice of the burrito (whose lines are spoken by a guy offstage and broadcast through a speaker next to the pedestal). At the end of its list of complaints about the transformation of San Francisco, the burrito says, "My aspirations hurt," and then, "Hold me close." The formidably serious-looking Yanez waltzes offstage, dancing cheek to cheek with this food item that was never true Mexican cuisine but a North American innovation, a fine symbol for a place that was always complex, hybrid, cross-cultural. Yanez's rapport with the burrito is painfully funny—what's being lost was only a burrito, a slightly scruffy neighborhood, not so perfect, not so transcendental, but it's wrenching to lose it all the same. Yanez himself—who fellow performance artist Guillermo Gómez-Peña introduced as "the capo, the godfather of three generations of Mission District artists"—is probably going to lose his home. His landlord had died since last I spoke with him, and so the building will probably be sold; and buildings that are sold are worth more if they've been emptied out—"delivered vacant." The artist Deborah Iyall, a Native American who was at the Alcatraz occupation decades ago, whose band Romeo Void made a splash in early 1980s punk rock, who made a solo reputation as a spoken-word artist, and who teaches printmaking to inner-city kids at the South of Market Cultural Center, has just called it quits and will be moving to Palm Desert. Even my collaborator, Susan Schwartzenberg, and the rest of the radicals in her Market Street building—including Chris Carlsson, the Steelworkers Union, and the Bike Coalition—look like they might be out of a workplace soon: the new owners have just sent them all a letter about the dynamic new plans they have for the building, which may be coded language for "the dotcoms are coming." Half of San Francisco seems to be going to insanely extravagant dot-com parties, and the other half seems to be mourning, dreading, and moving away.

Seattle is undergoing a similar tech-induced boom: a recent cover story of the *Seattle Weekly* read, "Will the Last Artist to Leave Seattle Please Turn Out the Lights," and comparable examples could be found in formerly great cities across the country. At the June 2000 United States Conference of Mayors, prosperity emerged as a widespread urban problem. As the *New York Times* puts it, "The booming urban economies have transformed places that were in a near-triage situation, but have made it harder for the poor and lower middle class to live in the cities." The *Times* cites Secretary of Housing and Urban Development Andrew Cuomo: "The urban boom has driven up home prices at twice the rate of inflation" so that "the federal government would have to step up its housing subsidies for the cities that are now pricing out low- and middle-wage job earners."[1] San Francisco is only an extreme case.

At Yanez's performance, City Lights editor Elaine Katzenberg remarks that the loss of artists because of the real estate frenzy feels oddly like the loss of artists during the darkest days of AIDS. The available analogies are countless. For a long time, I thought of 1950s science-fiction movies such as *Invasion of the Body Snatchers,* where aliens come and take over a community, though the movies were allegories for communist invasion, and it's capitalism unbound that San Franciscans are contending with. Sometimes I thought it was like the Gold Rush, when the Native Californians and Californios woke up to discover that their homes were in the way of a new economic explosion, though it was more complicated than that—some of the indignation of white bohemians seems to be that they expected always to be the settlers but woke up one day to find that they'd become the Indians. Environmental analogies fit best: someone like René Yanez is an endangered species whose habitat is drying up—drying up because there's no place to go that offers the same possibilities, and this habitat is being made over into something less complex and more commercial. Think of San Francisco as a rainforest being razed to grow a monocrop. Think of all the eccentrics and idealists as the forty species of orchids or as butterflies whose function is subtle but critical to the ecosystem. When rainforests are clearcut or burned to grow monocrops, they are productive for a few years, and then the soil gives out and what was once teaming with life becomes barren. San Francisco looks as though it is heading in that direction: having undermined bohemia, landlords and developers are now displacing restaurants, galleries, and even doctors and dentists for dot-coms; but who wants to live in a city without culture, food or medical care? The term *relic species* keeps coming to mind: a relic species is not extinct but its habitat is so severely compromised that it is due to become so. There are still artists and activists here, but the circumstances to generate more are doubtful at present, and it's not my peers and elders but the young I worry about; if San Francisco's bohemia were an ecosystem with biodiversity, the issue is sustainability.

Andrew, proprietor of the invitingly shabby Adobe Books, a fixture on 16th Street since the late 1980s that has given many young artists their first shows, says the young who come into his store now all have regular jobs: "They're better dressed. But they're not as well read." Still, when he has one of his periodic parties, the crowd is boisterous, overflowing onto the broad sidewalk and as scruffy as I remember from the past decade of Adobe parties. It's a party for Chris Johnson, a young artist who has had a small book of his drawings printed. Because only a few advance copies have actually arrived, he has hung them from the light fixtures, where they dangle like tiny piñatas: people grab one, peruse it, and let it go swinging through the hordes again as the band plays on. Out on the sidewalk I run

"A Rising Tide Lifts All Boats": Aaron Noble taking down the ark in his mural for and with Creativity Explored, an arts organization for the disabled, 2000.

into Aaron Noble, who's my age—thirty-eight—and ask him how things are going. The answer is not so good: his elderly landlord, like René's, has died, and his two-story industrial building is going to be demolished and replaced with a four-story condo complex, "maybe on the live/work model." Since it's only a block and a half away, he takes me over to tour his digs on Clarion Alley, between two worlds of Valencia and Mission Streets. Clarion was an alley infamous for crack and heroin, and so Noble, Michael O'Connor, scion of an old Mission District Irish family, and some other painters turned the whole alley into a mural project whose styles are entirely different from the Mission's dominant daughter-of-Diego-Rivera style. We walk down the dark alley, where people are still dealing drugs and smoking something at the far end, and he shows me the various contributions, including Castano's doorway depicting salsa singer Celia Cruz looking sexy in a tight pink dress, work by the now well-known Barry McGee, and his own "Superhero Warehouse" project with Rigo, depicting a Mondrian-style grid whose white spaces have become cells in which Marvel Comics heroes crouch.

We go into the building, which is a real live/work loft, an only moderately converted building that has housed artists since the 1960s and is rumored to have been built for the Industrial Workers of the World early in the twentieth century. Aaron's roommate Marisa Hernandez, a well-known local artist herself, is sitting on the sofa watching TV, and most of the space is filled with artworks, art materials, activist props, paintings—the arsenal of bohemia. When the building is torn down, the murals will go with them. The nightmare is that everything Noble has worked on in the past five years is vulnerable to erasure by redevelopment or new ownership. He was the director of the labor-history mural project in the Redstone Building, the former Labor Temple on Sixteenth Street that now houses dozens of social-issues and arts nonprofits but is up for sale, and a third project is on a site that will be redeveloped. His home of ten years and his work of the last five years could be wiped out as though he had never existed, never made a contribution, never learned to paint, never cared about his community. For people like Yanez and Noble, eviction is traumatic, but when they go they can take bohemia with them; they have become its incarnation, have internalized it. Being exiled from bohemia is one thing; never getting in is another. The admission fees keep getting higher and higher, and if a city is its people rather than its infrastructure, the city that counts won't be there for future generations to learn from, or to revolt against. It's the young I worry about, and so I set out to survey the generations.

"Delivered vacant" is a catch-phrase I learned from the sheaves of faxes from real estate agents accumulated by twenty-eight-year-old artist Nellie King Solomon in her hunt for housing. "It means they've already butchered the meat, so you can buy it shrinkwrapped in a neat little Styrofoam tray and not think about where it came from," says Solomon wryly, and she refused to consider the places where the realtors or sellers promised that tenants would be evicted for her. One flat was covered with signs saying "Please don't evict us," and Nellie won't but somebody will. "The savagery out there is incredible," she added. Daughter of four generations of San Francisco women—her great-grandmother arrived in the 1870s—Solomon went away for eight years to get out from under the long shadows of her well-known parents. A couple of years ago she came home—and this was home, she told me, the place she wanted to be, needed to be, where she had friends going back to childhood, knew the streets, the textures of walls. She had come home summers before, and it had always been easy to find a sublet or a short-term situation with roommates, but this time it was different. As a graduate student, she couldn't compete when it came to getting leases, and the roommate situations

Sam Chase, "Attack of the Yuppies," a poster for the How I Saved San Francisco bus shelter poster project, 2000. Inner City Public Arts Projects for Youth, sponsored by Artspan and SomArts.

had become far scarcer and stranger. She ended up moving back into her mother's small Telegraph Hill home for more than a year, entering a series of sublets, and looking for a place to buy with her share of the proceeds from the sale of her grandmother's Russian Hill home—thus the faxes. All through the writing of this book we talked about the city and our places in it.

I went to see Solomon's solo show at the California College of Arts and Crafts—a ravishing minimalist take on pointillism, with huge sheets of vellum whose dots sometimes looked like salmon scales and sometimes spelled out barely recognizable landscapes (including one that turned out to be the view through the tunnel on Treasure Island, between the San Francisco and Oakland halves of the Bay Bridge). We sat on the window-sill and talked while she waited for a photographer to come, and she told me that her year of househunting might be up: she had just bitten the bullet and put the winning bid on a flat in the lower Haight for somewhat less than half a million dollars, a sum that even with her grandmother's gift would make her have to work hard for money for the foreseeable future. It was, she said, the only way she could stay in San Francisco, and San Francisco was the only place she wanted to be. We compared our life-styles, for mine has been shaped to a significant degree by hanging onto a small apartment whose low rent has set me free to work hard at things that often pay little or nothing (if I lose my perch, I will face the standard choices: give up living in the Bay Area or give up my real work to get a lucrative job, which might be easier in terms of sheer workload but isn't what my life is for). "For my generation," Solomon told me, bohemianism "isn't an option, it's an ideal." Aaron Noble and I caught the last train to bohemia—or as he put it, "I rode into town on a horse called punk." The expanses of time in which we figured out ourselves and our work are no longer available to someone in such a city center: Solomon spoke of the

Giau Huynh, "Eviction Notice," a poster for the How I Saved San Francisco bus shelter poster project, 2000. Inner City Public Arts Projects for Youth, sponsored by Artspan and SomArts.

manic pace at which she did everything else to leave a little bit of time to work on her art, and when she did get to her school-supplied studio, she sometimes just lay down on the cool concrete floor.

Emily Miller is going on thirty and came to San Francisco from L.A. via the English Department at UC Berkeley. She was active during the Unity Front movement to improve the multicultural curriculum at the university, protested against the Gulf War, was one of the thousands of marchers during the Rodney King uprisings (up here, riots—that is, festivals of property destruction—were a small part of the activity), and most recently joined the local demonstrations in conjunction with the Washington, D.C., protests against the International Monetary Fund and World Bank. Working for the *San Francisco Bay Guardian,* our old-school-radical weekly, was her goal then, and she then went to work for a mainstream book publisher, at the usual entry-level starvation wage. Now, like thousands of other art and humanities majors, she is a dot-commer, an online editor and writer well past her first multimedia job. They've gained middle-class incomes—the bare minimum to stay afloat here—but they've lost their free time. She reminded me, though, that this new economy in which jobs are plentiful but housing is scarce is in some ways preferable to the one she graduated into, in the early 1990s, in which jobs were scarce and housing was more or less plentiful.

In a recent essay on *Underwire,* a 'Net magazine, she wrote about her adventures in the job market: "As I sat on a furry yellow beanbag, answering questions posed to me by a cheerful 24-year-old in jeans, I couldn't help but have a frightening flashback to my first real job interview. It was in 1994. I was wearing an ill-fitting black suit. I met with one book publishing executive after another, each one interrogating me on why they should condescend to hire me. I exhorted, I articulated, I groveled—in short I kissed some Donna Karan–covered ass for them to give me that job as

Assistant Editor, making about $20,000 … Back to the beanbag. My last interview was with an educational Web company. The perky 24-year-old … just stopped, looked at me and said, 'Isn't it cool that suddenly there are so many jobs for content types like us?' Yeah, I thought, it's bizarre, lucky, and very cool.… Times have changed. The strange thing now is seeing a new generation of upwardly mobile twentysomethings walk straight out of college and into great jobs at a dot.com making $50K a year. Sure, we could head into another recession, but by the time we do, they will already be firmly established in their careers. They'll never get to live through their young adulthood waiting tables at the Olive Garden or getting rejected by a temp agency. They'll never eat eggs and toast at 11 a.m. on a Tuesday with all their friends who are also out of work. And in a way, I feel sorry for them."[2]

Torn poster, Mission District, 2000.

Emily remembers when the brave new world of the Internet was more about "a lot of creative weirdos" than commerce, knows a former bike messenger who's "really down on this whole thing and she *is* a dot-comer." So who, I asked, are the people trying to run me over in the brand-new SUVs? "Oh, those are the biz-dev [business development] and the sales and marketing people," she quickly replied. "Those are some of the higher-paid people. The content people are from here; you don't get paid enough in content to do a cross-country move." And what, I asked, was the upside of the Internet? Emily listed "access for disabled people—an entire world where you can be anything you want; lots of jobs and some of them are jobs that are really fun; books for your friends in Iowa; instant messaging and e-mail, which are increasingly social-activist tools, and where I find out about small theater and a lot of arts information; Amazon.com—evil as it is, it carries a lot of books other people don't; Bibliofind is a huge good thing; empowered humanities majors; amazing for research, it's a great place for communicating with like-minded people, for illness research and community, though there's terrible misinformation on the Web; my husband's on the Renaissance art map online group, another community. . . . " Miller is for the Internet, and I can't imagine a champion whose integrity and reason are more convincing. She notes that many artists and writers are making a good living from it—but I would argue that what they're doing most often uses their skills without tapping into their idealism, and the reason they need to make a good living is because of the overall economic changes locally amplified by the Internet. What the Internet provides is one thing; what the Internet economy erodes is another.

Meanwhile, the Internet seems to be radically altering the cultural landscape in ways Miller didn't list. Like personal computers fifteen years earlier, the Internet both democratizes and consolidates. Desktop publishing was spectacularly valuable for small organizations, and the Internet has become a place to peddle, say, rap songs by artists too minor and radical to get a major-label release. But it's also increased the grasp of megacorporations. Amazon.com, for example, makes practically everything in print available to anyone who's online, but it is further undermining the viability of independent bookstores already ravaged by chain stores in the past decade. The Internet may make culturally enrich your life if you live in an utter backwater, and it has been an extraordinary tool for activists around the world to organize against everything from landmines to the World Trade Organization, but in many ways it makes life worse for those who live in the centers.[3] The Internet threatens to homogenize space and place by making what was once the center no more rich and lively than what was once the periphery.

All places being equal thus means that the very remoteness of wilderness and the very centrality of cities will be undone, that space will no longer have texture or meaning, and we will no longer be motivated to move through it. And this brings us to the most pernicious effect of the new technology: its hostility to public life. The rhetoric of the new technology constantly celebrates liberation from the need to leave the house, or, if we do leave the house, to learn to navigate, to ask strangers for directions or other acts of connection made obsolete by GPS and cell phones (and encounters with those who have no house to leave). The promise that we will no longer have to enter the world in order to get commodities and information at the very least overvalues commodities and information and undervalues getting out into the world. This is a promise that we will no longer have to negotiate spatially or socially; getting means clicking boxes and typing in credit card numbers (though, as Calvin Welch pointed out to me, the commodities get driven around anyway: online sales still require warehouses and trucks, warehouse workers and truck drivers).

Both wilderness and urban public space are about life that is for other things, for encounter, experience, the successful navigation of risk and mystery, the knowledge that cannot be bought or sold, for membership in biological and political communities; for the possibility of participation. The Internet can be for communication and information, but it is an increasingly commercial territory, and its transformation of a real city must be taken into account as one of its attributes. Is it a coincidence that the Internet economy has moved in on and begun to homogenize one of the most distinctive, eclectic and highly textured places in the world? The San Francisco writer and renegade programmer Ellen Ullman asserts that the infinite variety the Internet offers means that people can tailor countless selections to their individual taste, with an emphasis on *individual*—on the atomized individual no longer participating in public life or public dialogue, no longer a citizen, only a stay-at-home consumer of products and information so selective they no longer form a common ground or even a conversational possibility with others. She concludes, "The Net ideal represents a retreat not only from political life but also from culture—from that tumultuous conversation in which we try to talk to one another about our shared experiences. . . . Whether or not we come to an agreement or an understanding, even if some decide that understanding and meaning are impossible, we are still sitting around the same campfire. But the Web as it has evolved is based on the idea that we do not even want a shared experience."[4]

For those of us who have had our decades of development in San Francisco, exile is a tragedy of the heart, but not of the mind: someone like René Yanez embodies San Francisco, even characters like Noble and me have got what we need from the city and can take it with us. The 28-year-olds are digging in their heels, though what it takes for them to stay looks exhausting and compromising to me. It's the eighteen-year-olds I worry about most. If they can find a niche at all in San Francisco they will find it in a city sadly reduced in mentors, role models, options and eccentrics. And they know it. The going-on-eighteen-year-olds I met in Jennifer Wofford's class at Leadership High, a small charter school, would look like a glorious future if they had an assured arena in which to carry it out. The 28-year-old Wofford, a sculptor and a member of the Mail Order Brides, a trio of Filipina-American artists with a sharp sense of humor, was born in San Francisco but raised in the burbs, came back to study at the San Francisco Art Institute, and stayed. As I talk to her students about the Internet, she remarks at one point that everyone in her generation has sold out, using their skills to make stuff that definitely is not art. She herself loves teaching high school and bought a house in rough West Oakland so she could continue.

I had seen her students' art before I met them: fellow Filipina artist Joanna Poethig, a long-time community arts activist and muralist who had also just bought a house in Oakland, had done a city-sponsored poster project with several of them. The theme of the posters was "How I Saved San Francisco." It was, Poethig said, a way to introduce visual culture to media-saturated kids, and so was billed as the superstar in an imaginary movie. Giau Huyh was in "America's #1 Movie: Eviction Notice." She loomed like a friendly Leviathan over a tall building, with the words "saves homeless," "homegirlz," and "25 days left" scattered on the poster. Vincente Nalam had used the Tagalog word *Manghihlot* as the title for his vibrant green poster, with the subtitles "The Healer of Natoma Street" and "He heals the lost souls of San Francisco with his white light." He too hovered over a building, but as a mother bird hovers over the nest, not as King Kong loomed over Manhattan. Another poster was titled "Jazzy and Samantha in The Do Right Girls: Our Eyes Stop Violence." Poethig told me that the Tenderloin kids were concerned with homelessness and community, the African-American kids with violence, and the Leadership High students with culture. Among the latter were Claire starring in the "Adventures of Clarin-Hood," in which she "takes from the cruel clothes corporation and gives back to the sweatshop worker," and Sam, whose poster said "Sam vs the Attack of the Yuppies. Will He Make San Francisco Frappuccino free?" The posters will eventually appear in the Gannett-owned Muni bus shelters, which give nonprofits poster space as part of their agreement with the city (the rest of the time, the shelters feature ads for everything from whiskey to clothes to, of course, dot-coms).

Wofford's kids, most of whom were born here, were as grumpy about what was happening to their city as anyone. Diversity, they all quickly said, was what made San Francisco valuable to them, and diversity seemed to be on its way out. Only Eduardo didn't have much good to say about San Francisco, though what he deplored seemed to have as much to do with living in a dark apartment looking out onto other apartments as with the city as a whole. A lot of them didn't see a future for themselves here and scorned the idea of dot-com jobs. What's missing from the Internet? I asked, and chartreuse-haired Sam and shave-headed Eduardo immediately said, "Life." Despite their dour comments, they, like Wofford and maybe because of her, seemed to regard life as an often-hilarious adventure, though unlike her they hadn't really faced its practical problems yet and couldn't really speak to them. They have enough facing them already. Leadership High School is losing its perch within Golden Gate University, a small law and business school downtown. It's being evicted, and though rated third among the city's high schools, it is not receiving district help in relocating. Its classrooms on First Street will probably be rented to dot-coms.

Civic Center demonstration, August 2000.

Cities are the infrastructure of shared experience. Thirty years ago we worried that cities were being abandoned to desperate poverty and decay. Even five years ago the threat seemed to be redesign and new development that eliminated public space and public life, a suburbanization by design. No one foresaw that cities could be abandoned to the ravages of wealth, or that public life and public space could be undermined by acceleration and privatization of everyday life, by spatial practices rather than the alteration of actual space. Something utterly unpredictable has happened to cities: they have flourished, with a vengeance, but by ceasing to be cities in the deepest sense. Are they becoming a city-shaped suburb for the affluent? Will the chaotic and diverse form of the city be preserved, but with its content smoothed out, homogenized by wealth? San Francisco could become a hollow city, a Disneyland of urbanism in which its varicolored Victorian houses and diversity of skin colors and cuisines covers up the absence of the poor, the subversive, the creative, the elderly, the free. In a way, all of San Francisco is being delivered vacant to the brave new technology economy, and altruism and idealism are two of the tenants facing homelessness. It is clear that the Internet economy won't continue to boom as wildly as it has, but it is here to stay. Of course, the technology only extends the reach of a capitalist agenda that began privatizing the public and maximizing the commodification of everyday life long ago.

Civic Center demonstration, August 2000.

Activists seem better able to stay here than artists, in part because the former are the ultimate organizers and collectivists dealing with bottom-line issues, while the latter are, as Debra Walker deplored, most often individualists until it's too late. Too, activists have managed to buy a number of houses in which they live collectively. But many of them are on their way out as well—it's one thing to economize by making every room in a flat but the kitchen into someone's bedroom, and it's another to find such a flat for rent in the almost zero-vacancy, intensely competitive renters' market. Activist workspaces are at least as threatened as affordable housing. In a recent survey, 50 percent of the nonprofits surveyed had leases due to expire by the end of 2000, 70 percent within the next three years. Rent on these spaces can increase as much as 600 percent, putting many organizations out of business, and though some are working on global or national issues that can be addressed from other locations, many are working with vulnerable populations in the immediate community and cannot continue from afar.[5] Activism is being squeezed on both ends: by losing its workspace and by losing housing that activists can afford, and the repercussions will be colossal. On the front lines, immigrants, sweatshop workers, the mentally and physically ill, battered women, homeless

people, at-risk youth will lose their defenders and care providers; beyond that immediate population of sufferers is the impact San Francisco's progressives have had on the nation since the nineteenth century. This place has been one of the great laboratories for broadening and transforming our understanding of human rights, justice, economics, work, gender, sexuality, the natural world, as creative in its activism as its arts. For San Francisco to become a place that just provides opportunities to buy pet food online is, to say the least, a decline whose effects will be felt far away.

Civic Center demonstration, August 2000.

City officials might consider what constitutes prosperity as we lurch toward becoming a city where social services and service providers are priced out of the region; a city without daycare workers or firefighters is one version of hell, even if everyone in it is driving a Lincoln Navigator. Recently, the doctors and dentists in one downtown building and successful restaurants and major art galleries have been added to the list of the threatened species; bookstores are having a hard time finding employees who can and will work for bookstore wages; and student housing has become a crisis at both public and private colleges in San Francisco. The crisis has spread far beyond bohemia and the poor and is making inroads on established San Francisco. From a purely commercial point of view, it could be a disaster: San Francisco's main industry is still tourism, and though the Golden Gate Bridge and the hills are here to stay, much of the subtler charm tourists come for—alternative culture, lively clubs, interesting characters—could trickle away. Even at its worst, even as the nadir of public life, tourism is still about public life: about walking around, encountering the unknown, feeling the textures that make places distinctive. Those who keep the tourism economy running are salespeople, hotel and restaurant workers, and they too are being priced out of the city and perhaps the region.[6] San Francisco hotels are said to have become so expensive that the city is losing its appeal to vacation travelers, if not to business travelers. A developer tells me that dot-coms are moving into Fisherman's Wharf, completing its passage through the peristaltic American economy: from a place of food production with all the risks and sensory aspects such labor can provide; to a tourist site celebrating that food and labor; to another white-collar worksite for an information economy that could be located anywhere—Silicon Wharf, the developer notes, is its nickname. Meanwhile, a dot-com has leased the top floor of the Cannery, the fruit and seafood canning factory whose 1967 conversion into a mall set the style for such conversions around the country.[7] These transformations could be read as the return of labor after an interlude of leisure or as a further deterioration of the life of the senses and the further homogenization of the world.

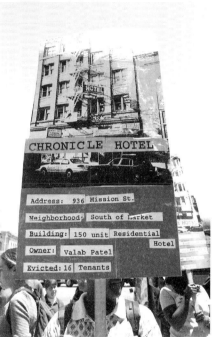

Civic Center demonstration, August 2000.

Late in the game, coalitions are forming to fight the hollowing out of San Francisco. There had been flurries of organizing and demonstrations at least since 1998, but in the summer of 2000 artists, activist and longtime affordable housing advocates began to exert real force and work with real unity. The coalitions that had disbanded after Ammiano's valiant mayoral campaign in late 1999 began to gather again to retake the city. The city came alive with outrage, and the most valuable aspects of it suddenly became as visible as they are vulnerable. The Mission Anti-Displacement Coalition and other groups put up striking mul-

ticolored posters around the neighborhood advertising demonstrations
and meetings, while scathingly funny posters about the issue appeared
across the Mission. Even the walls have woken up in this neighborhood,
and bits of graffiti and creative alteration adorn other areas as well, if not
so lavishly. Demonstrations flourished, nowhere more so than during the
August 2000 eviction of the Dancer's Group studio after eighteen years—
another defacto eviction caused by a huge rent increase (500 percent in
this case). Dancers refused to go, dozens of performances were held outside the occupied studio, and huge groups gathered in the street. Other
groups began to link displacement and globalization, and what in 1998
had only been a complaint-oriented conversation became a real political
analysis and response. It has never been easy to get citizens involved in the
undramatic minutia of urban planning, but when a city declines as visibly
as San Francisco, it's possible.

Proposition M has come back with a vengeance as the Office Development Controls Initiative, Proposition L, cosponsored by Debra Walker
and supported by Ammiano and Calvin Welch, among many others, a
measure so effective that Mayor Willie Brown tried to keep it off the
ballot, held huge fundraisers for his own competing, business-as-usual
proposition, and fired the one planning commissioner who supported
Prop. L. Beginning with a proposal to "link commercial development to
transit capacity and improvements, and discourage displacement of community services and arts activities," it classifies Internet and computer
businesses as "office space" and live/work units as "dwelling units," closing the loopholes that let such businesses and homes colonize without
controls or contributions. Yet more radically, the initiative requires that
environmental impact reports "address the economic and social effects
of a project on the demand for housing, and displacement of affordable
housing, community services, small businesses, and arts and cultural insti-

tutions" and directs the Board of Supervisors to consider "requiring office developers to dedicate 10 percent of the floor space in projects in excess of 50,000 square feet to non-profit organizations providing community services."[8] Many of these ideas appeared earlier in the Political Ecology Group's platform, written as part of a project to organize nonprofits under the umbrella People Against Displacement. But so much of what was once San Francisco will have hemorrhaged away before measures like Proposition L can be implemented.

The proposed solutions recall environmentalism long ago, when it was the conservation movement: it sought to preserve wildernesses, intact ecosystems and endangered species within a society that was devouring the landscape for development and resource extraction. These places and creatures became islands risen up above the tide of greed. When it became clear that creating exceptions to the rules was no longer an adequate solution, conservationists began asking larger questions about those rules and became environmentalists: they recognized that only profound changes in priorities and practices would sustain the ecosystems we depend upon. In the best of the save-San-Francisco scenarios outlined above, nonprofits, artists and activists would also become protected preserves and species in a system that no longer willingly accommodates their survival; they will have been conserved, but as islands in a hostile sea.

For idealists and visionaries to become endangered themselves could create a huge chain reaction. Of course, on another scale San Francisco—as Food First, Global Exchange, Planet Drum, Rainforest Action Network, Urban Ecology, the International Indian Treaty Council—is asking larger questions and making larger demands on that system. But apocalyptic scenarios are tidy solutions disguised as the ultimate problem. Creative and activist life is not coming to an end, but the circumstances encouraging it are in rapid decline, in San Francisco and in the nation at large. Such a decline raises questions about why in times of such abundance there is not enough to go around, why the quality of life is going down as wealth shoots up, why in what's supposed to be a boom economy the instabilities and unaffordabilities that created the homeless are encroaching on those who used to be middle class. These are some of the larger questions, in San Francisco and across America, about greed, shortsightedness and the distribution of power and resources. This time around, the answers could be surprising.

Notes

San Francisco, Capital of the Twenty-First Century

Note that by the time of publication, all the statistics cited will be historical. Everything from home prices to the numbers of evictions seems to have increased since these figures were gathered.

1. Thirty-four percent of the venture capital: Bay Area Economic Forum, *Winning in the Global Economy*, September 1999, p. 13. This report states in its opening pages, "If it were an independent country, the Bay Area would constitute the world's 21st-largest economy, bigger than Sweden or Austria. The Bay Area is the global economy productivity leader in the knowledge-intensive business clusters of telecommunications, computers and electronics, bioscience, multimedia, and environmental technology. The Bay Area is second only to New York in its number of *Fortune* 500 headquarters. The Bay Area has moved to first from second in income per capital at $38,300 ahead of New York at $35,900.... The Bay Area has the second-highest cost of living among comparative regions. This is largely the result of sharply increased housing prices driven by rising wages, equity-rich buyers, and a worsening housing supply shortage, particularly for lower-income housing. Traffic congestion in the Bay Area has significantly worsened...." (from fact-sheet on pp. 5–6). So much for the city of fruits and nuts. Thirty percent of the Internet/multimedia: Bay Area Economic Forum website as of April 2000.

2. Thirty percent is a very modest figure: According to Carol Emert, *San Francisco Chronicle*, May 26, 2000: "Median Bay Area home prices rose to $358,000 in April, up 22.6 percent from April 1999 and 4.7 percent from last March, according to DataQuick." Randy Shaw cites 37 percent in James Brook, Chris Carlsson, and Nancy Peters, eds., *Reclaiming San Francisco* (San Francisco: City Lights Books, 1998), 300. A 20 percent figure for Potrero Hill, for example, was cited in *San Francisco Examiner*, "Impossible Dream," B-1, May 5, 2000.

3. Bay Area Economic Forum, *Pulse*, Spring 1999, p. 1 (available online).

4. More than seven reported evictions a day probably means several times as many are taking place. San Francisco's rent control limits the grounds for eviction, and owner move-ins are one of the remaining legal causes, though many times the owner doesn't actually reside there for the specified time before moving in a new tenant at a greatly increased rent. Katherine Seligman, "Fighting to Call a Place Home," *San Francisco Examiner,* October 25, 1999: "Owner move-in eviction notices have more than tripled in the past three years, going from 420 in 1995 to 1,301 last year, according to city records. But an *Examiner* analysis of 1998 figures shows the numbers are rising even faster this year, the result of a buying craze prompted in part by pending legal restrictions. There were 983 owner move-in eviction notices during the first six months of 1998. At that rate, the *Examiner* found, The City may see more than 1,900 by year's end—an average of five tenants evicted every day." The *Bay Guardian,* May 24, 2000, lists 2,641 reported evictions in 1999 and "only a fraction of evictions are filed with the city"—more than seven a day. San Francisco Tenants' Union reports that 70 percent of those evicted leave San Francisco.

5. As of June 1999 there were 47,000 high-tech/Internet workers, according to an article in the *Potrero View* ("Multimedia Boom: Hill Braces for the Big Squeeze," April 2000), which in a city of approximately 800,000 means nearly 1 out of 16 people is employed in the industry (and given that a significant portion of the overall population—seniors, children—doesn't work, the percentage of the workforce in high-tech is significantly higher). The city's survey is reported in Ilana DeBare, "S.F. Job Market Jumping," *San Francisco Chronicle,* January 22, 1999.

6. Urban Habitat Program, San Francisco, *There Goes the Neighborhood: A Regional Analysis of Gentrification and Community in the San Francisco Bay Area,* 1999, p. iii.

7. Jeff Goodell, "Down and Out in Silicon Valley," *Rolling Stone*, December 9, 1999.

8. Neil Smith and Peter Williams, "Gentrification of the City," quoted in *If You Lived Here: The City in Art, Theory and Social Activism,* a project by Martha Rosler, Brian Wallis, ed. (New York: Dia Foundation for the Arts, 1991), 148.

9. William Saunders, editor of *Harvard Design Magazine*, "Is Up-Scale a Downer? The Gentrification and Globalization of Harvard Square," MS for *Boston Globe* editorial handed to the author in April 2000.

10. Paul Rauber, *East Bay Express*, December 24, 1999.

11. American Indian Contemporary Arts' eviction was covered by the *San Francisco Chronicle* and, on December 15, 1999, by the *San Francisco Bay Guardian,* which reports that the rent went from the $3,500 AICA paid to the $10,000 per month that new tenant Financial Interactive will pay. As of June 2000, the AICA is homeless.

12. *Wall Street Journal*, March 2, 2000, quoted in *S.F. Weekly.*

13. Rexroth, quoted in Bruce Cook, *The Beat Generation* (New York: Charles Scribner, 1971), p. 28.

14. Carey McWilliams, *California: The Great Exception* (Berkeley: University of California Press, 1999 [1949], 139).

15. Richard DeLeon, *Left Coast City: Progressive Politics in San Francisco, 1975–1991* (Lawrence: University Press of Kansas, 1992), 14–15.

The Shopping Cart and the Lexus

1. Albert S. Broussard, *Black San Francisco: The Struggle for Racial Equality in the West, 1900–1954* (Lawrence: University Press of Kansas, 1993), on segregation and the ninefold increase of the African-American population, 133, 205; "Blacks occupied a disproportionate share….": 173–74.

2. Linda Hamalian, *A Life of Kenneth Rexroth* (New York: Norton, 1991), 112–14.

3. Angelou, *I Know Why the Caged Bird Sings* (New York: Random House, 1969), 203–4.

4. Michael McClure, conversation with the author, November 1999.

5. Leonard S. Mosias for the San Francisco Redevelopment Agency, "Residential Rehabilitation Survey Western Addition Area 2," July 1962, unpaginated.

6. San Francisco Redevelopment Agency, "Report on the Redevelopment Plan for the Western Addition Approved Redevelopment Project Area A-2," July 21, 1964, 2; statistics on following pages.

7. Broussard, *Black San Francisco*, 94.

8. Eric Foner and John A. Garraty, *The Reader's Companion to American History* (New York: Houghton Mifflin, 1991), 176.

9. Eric Fang,"Urban Renewal Revisited: A Design Critique," SPUR (San Francisco Planning and Urban Research Association) website essay. Fang is an architect and a member of SPUR's urban policies committee.

10. Chester Hartman, *The Transformation of San Francisco* (Towota, N.J.: Rowman and Allanheld, 1984), 19.

11. Hartman, *Transformation of San Francisco,* 13.

12. Calvin Welch, in conversation with the author, March 2000.

13. See the essay by my brother David Solnit, a co-organizer of the tours, on the *Reshaping San Francisco* CD-ROM produced by Chris Carlsson and mentioned in Lucy Lippard's *On the Beaten Track*.

14. For more on the I-Hotel struggle, see James Sobredo, "From Manila Bay to Daly City: Filipinos in San Francisco," in James Brook, Chris Carlsson and Nancy Peters, *Reclaiming San Francisco: History, Politics, Culture* (San Francisco: City Lights Books, 1998).

15. Anders Corr, *No Trespassing: Squatting, Rent Strikes, and Land Struggles Worldwide* (Boston: South End Press, 1999), 18.

16. Ruth Glass, cited in Neil Smith, *The New Urban Frontier: Gentrification and the Revanchist City* (London: Routledge, 1996), 32.

17. Brian Godfrey, *Neighborhoods in Transition: The Making of San Francisco's Ethnic and Nonconformist Communities* (Berkeley: University of California Press, 1988), 177–78

18. Randy Shilts, quoted in Godfrey, ibid., 121.

19. Godfrey, ibid., 121.

20. *San Francisco Bay Guardian*, "Neighborhood Profile: The Mission/Lofts and Lattes" in the special issue "The Economic Cleansing of San Francisco," October 7, 1998, 20.

21. Neil Smith,*The New Urban Frontier*, 32–33

A Real Estate History of the Avant-Garde

1. Jason B. Johnson, "Mission Bay Development Plans Unveiled," *San Francisco Chronicle,* August 26, 1998: "The project would include . . . 6,090 housing units. Mission Bay will create 938 construction jobs annually, and add 42,000 permanent jobs to the city's workforce when it is completed, officials said." Also see Carl Nolte, *Chronicle,* October 25, 1999: "If everything planned is built, UC San Francisco and Mission Bay together will contain 8.1 million square feet of office and research space— enough to fill 15 Transamerica Pyramids. Not to mention 6,000 new housing units, 700,000 square feet of stores and entertainment spaces and a 500-room hotel."

2. Gray Brechin, in a talk about his book *Imperial San Francisco: Urban Power, Earthly Ruin* (University of California Press, 1999) and in conversation with the author. Also see Angela Rowen,"Dangerous Mission," *San Francisco Bay Guardian,* September 23, 1998: "In fact, evidence suggests that . . . the Mission Bay development will drive up housing prices throughout the southeast sector of the city. A study released by San Francisco State's Urban Institute suggests that escalating prices will force low-income residents of Bayview-Hunters Point and Potrero Hill to move."

3. Rachel Gordon, *San Francisco Examiner*, October 20, 1998.

4. Oscar Lewis, *The Big Four* (New York: Knopf, 1938), 264.

5. Henri Murger, *Latin Quarter*, trans. Elizabeth Ward Hugus (and retitled from *Scenes de la vie de bohème*) (New York and Hartford: Edwin Valentine Mitchell, and Dodd, Mead and Co, 1930), 2.

6. Ibid., 3.

7. Ibid., 31.

8. Though Murger was largely apolitical, he tosses off expressions such as "He beat a quick retreat from the Luxembourg humming quietly a sentimental ballad which was for him the Marseillaise of Love," ibid. p. 44.

9. Shelley Rice, *Parisian Views* (Cambridge, Mass.: MIT Press, 1997), 34–35.

10. Lewis, Edmond and Jules De Goncourt, *The Goncourt Journals, 1851–1870,* trans. Lewis Galantiere (New York: Doubleday, 1937), 93. It's worth remembering that the Goncourts were reactionaries who in an unquoted part of this passage objected to the expansion of the public arena and attacked Murger extensively, out of a sort of class loathing for this successful tailor's son.

11. T. J. Clark, *The Painting of Modern Life* (Princeton, N.J.: Princeton University Press, 1984), 51.

12. Franklin Dickerson Walker, *San Francisco's Literary Frontier* (Seattle: University of Washington, 1970).

13. Nancy S. Peters and Lawrence Ferlinghetti, *Literary San Francisco: A Pictorial History from Its Beginnings to the Present Day* (San Francisco: City Lights Books and Harper and Row), 60.

14. Diego Rivera with Gladys March, *My Art, My Life: An Autobiography* (New York: Dover 1991 [1960]), 105, 106.

15. Anthony W. Lee, *Painting on the Left: Diego Rivera, Radical Politics, and San Francisco's Public Murals* (Berkeley: University of California Press, 1999), 23.

16. Walter Benjamin, "The Author as Producer," *Reflections* (New York: Harcourt Brace Jovanovich, 1986), 222.

17. Michael McClure, "San Francisco Was a Hotbed," in Rebecca Solnit, *Secret Exhibition: Six California Artists of the Cold War Era* (San Francisco: City Lights Books, 1990), 26–27.

18. McClure, conversation with the author, November 1999.

19. Bruce Conner, conversation with the author, March 11, 2000.

20. McClure, ibid.

21. Richard Candida Smith, *Utopia and Dissent: Art, Poetry and Politics in California* (Berkeley: University of California Press, 1995), 80.

22. Richard Walker, conversation with the author, March 2000.

23. Richard Walker, "An Appetite for the City," in Brook, Carlsson and Peters, *Reclaiming San Francisco*, 9.

24. Calvin Welch, conversation with the author, March 2000

25. David Antin, keynote talk at the San Francisco Art Institute's annual summer criticism conference, August 1988. Tape courtesy of Bill Berkson.

26. Joan Holden, conversation with the author, March 2000.

27. Debra Walker, conversation with the author, March 2000.

28. Coalition on Jobs, Art and Housing website, March 2000.

29. Tyche Hendricks, "Hotseat" feature, *San Francisco Examiner,* June 24, 1999.

30. Debra Walker in conversation with the author, March 2000.

31. René Yanez, conversation with the author, March 16, 2000.

32. See, for example, *Harper's* Index for July 2000: "Number of U.S. counties in which a full-time minimum-wage earner can afford a one-bedroom apartment: 0"; or countless articles on the unaffordability of housing for greater and greater portions of the population. Again, San Francisco is only an extreme version of a pervasive problem.

33. Lawrence Rinder in a July 23, 1999, panel discussion organized by the *San Francisco Chronicle*, which published his talk on November 15, 1999.

Skid Marks on the Social Contract

1. Baudelaire, "Eyes of the Poor," *Paris Spleen,* trans. Louise Varese (New York: New Directions, 1947), 52–53.

2. *The Independent,* May 16, 2000, 12A, in a story about a hearing where neighbors—almost all from the same condo complex—are trying to shut down the Maritime Hall, one of the last major venues for punk and other alternative kinds of music in the city.

3. *Noe Valley Voice*, April 2000.

4. Pedestrian statistics from SPUR (San Francisco Planning and Urban Research Association) website sustainability page: " In the 1997–1998 time period, there were 2,200 auto–pedestrian collisions—3 per day! And in 1996, there were 21 pedestrian deaths—a figure that shockingly grew almost 50% to 30 deaths in 1998."

5. Kevin Keating, conversation with the author, March 2000.

6. Mike Weiss, "'70s Lifestyle vs. Dot-Com": "Silicon Valley is zapping S.F.'s cultural revolution. The mayoral race between Willie Brown and Tom Ammiano is a symbol of the battle between two life-styles in the new San Francisco," *San Francisco Chronicle,* December 9, 1999, p. 1.

7. Phillip Matier and Andrew Ross, *San Francisco Chronicle,* November 1, 1999.

8. See *Independent,* April 8, 2000, cover story, and various stories in the *San Francisco Chronicle,* including April 13, p. A19.

9. Carol Lloyd: "I'm the enemy! At a meeting of San Franciscans trying to stop gentrification, I realize that I'm the Internet yuppie scum that's ruining my neighborhood!" October 29, 1999, *Salon* magazine. She took up the same sidetracking arguments in a May 9, 2000, SFGate (*San Francisco Chronicle* online) piece titled "Avant-Garde Artist Dot-Conned Out of Alley."

Amnesia Is a Club

1. Nick Kozloff, conversation with the author, March 2000. Kozloff is a pseudonyn used at the artist's request—in part to protect his rent-controlled New York apartment.

2. Kenneth Dowlin, letter to the editor, *San Francisco Chronicle,* June 22, 1996.

3. Gray Brechin, letter to the editor, *San Francisco Chronicle,* June 6, 1996. See also Nicholson Baker's October 14, 1996, article in the *New Yorker* and another version of his manifesto on the value of card catalogues in his essay collection *The Size of Thoughts.*

4. Susan Miller, conversation with the author, March 2000. The photographer Kate Joyce wrote me of an encounter while she was photographing Starbucks for this book: "Down on Mariposa, next door to Cell Space is one such undercover Buckaroo, called Circadia Coffee House. While photographing the building I met two men out front having a Marlboro/Starbucks, nicotine/caffeine break from their Internet job on 18th St. They come every day, and the man on the left with an English accent went on to say, 'If it weren't for the money in this city I wouldn't be here,' to which his dot-com companion affirmed [that] you just 'make the money and get out.'"

Delivered Vacant

1. Timothy Egan, "Urban Mayors Share the (Not Unwelcome) Burden of Coping with Prosperity," *New York Times,* June 13, 2000. In *The Last Intellectuals,* Russell Jacoby writes of the 1950s, "The shrinking cultural space—acknowledged or unacknowledged—herded younger intellectuals into the university. If academic salaries and security were the carrot, the decline of traditional intellectual life was the stick.... This dwindling space is not only a metaphor; it denotes the loss of living areas, the renovation of urban bohemias into exclusive quarters of boutiques and townhouses.... Economic exingencies reshaped New York into a city of extremes, a city that could no longer sustain bohemians who were neither rich nor poor."

2. Emily Miller, "Dot.Com-A-Rama," *Underwire,* April 2000.

3. Amanda Nowinski, in a July 12, 2000, *Bay Guardian* article, enumerated a few of the recent losses:

"The Joe Goode Performance Group and Dancer's Group Studio Theater, which will leave its Mission locale Aug. 15, owing to a rent increase from $3,000 a month to $15,000; San Francisco Cinematheque, which moved from Potrero Avenue to Hunters Point June 1; RayKo South photo rental lab, which shut its doors June 30; Centro Social Obrero, a longtime labor hiring and Latino dance hall, closed June 24; S.F. Camerawork, which will move in with New Langton Arts because of an increase in rent from $30,000 to more than $110,000 a year; the music-rehearsal space Art Explosion (the group is still fighting its eviction in court); the Z Space Studio theater, whose rent is increasing by $100,000 a year; and ironically, the city's first computer art school, the Computer Arts Institute." Performer/choreographer and founder of 848 Community Space at 848 Divisadero (in a building up for sale), Keith Hennessy adds to the list: "Dancers' Group/Footwork: A dance studio since the 1950's, a major center for contemporary dance development since 1982, will be closed August 15. Rent went from $3,100 to $14,000. and the new owners, real estate speculators Pomegranate Design, claim that the 'market value' of the space is double what they offered," and "50 Oak. Largest dance school in the city. Several studios and home to Lines Ballet."

4. Ellen Ullman, "The Museum of Me," *Harper's*, May 2000, p. 33.

5. Statistics provided by the Political Ecology Group, San Francisco. See their draft manifesto, which begins, "San Franciscans rely on an estimated 800 non-profit community service organizations to provide desperately needed services, help us to express our voices and improve our overall quality of life. Recent studies from the Mayor's Office show that one-third of the city's community service organizations will be forced out of San Francisco by the end of this year, unless we act now. Greed by landlords, developers and realty speculators and lax compliance by city government in enforcing existing laws has led to an eviction epidemic for the organizations that serve us and make San Francisco unique."

6. See the Robin Davis, "Restaurant Service Losing Luster," *San Francisco Chronicle*, July 19, 2000: "With unemployment at an all-time low, many businesses are in the throes of labor woes, but perhaps none as much as the labor-intensive restaurant industry, a linchpin of the local economy. In San Francisco, restaurants made up 23 percent of the city's taxable sales in 1998, the latest year for which figures are available, according to the California Board of Equalization.... As with many other businesses, restaurant servers are fleeing to dot-coms, say general managers and restaurant owners."

7. Marianne Costantinou, "Cannery Top Floor Shifting to Dot-Coms," *San Francisco Examiner,* July 13, 2000.

8. Information from www.savesanfrancisco.org, July 2000.

Acknowledgements

With thanks to James V. Young, building manager, veteran, acquaintance of Bonnie and Clyde during his sharecropping youth in Oklahoma, who long ago invited Rebecca into her current residence, René Yanez, Paul Yamazaki and City Lights Books, Jennifer Wofford at Leadership High School and her students, Calvin Welch at the Council of Community Housing Organizations, Lewis Watts, Richard Walker, Debra Walker, the city's surviving vacant lots, the Robert Mitchum shrine in the women's room at Tosca's, Mr. Teal, Nellie Solomon, Charlie Schwartzenberg, the Seventeen Reasons Why sign at Seventeenth and Mission, the St. John Coltrane African Orthodox Church, Rigo, Joanna Poethig, the bar La Pigalle where the authors first compared notes on the ravaging of their city, Brenda O'Sullivan at Modern Times Books, Ira Nowinski, Aaron Noble, the Museé Mechanique and Giant Camera at the Cliff House, Susan Miller at New Langton Arts, Emily Miller, Michael McClure, Chip Lord, Kate Joyce, David Johnson, Rupert Jenkins, Annice Jacoby, Ludovic Ibarra, Joan Holden, Connie Hatch, Beth Hass, *Harvard Design Magazine,* which published an essay from which this book grew and particularly Rebecca's editor Nancy Levinson there, the corner of Gough and Fell where the Occult Bookstore confronts Walgreen's, Guillermo Gómez-Peña, the Exploratorium, Brad Erickson at the Political Ecology Group, Eric Drooker, Janet Delaney, Mike Davis, Critical Mass, Anders Corr, Clair Corcoran, the construction and demolition workers who welcomed Susan and her camera onsite, Bruce Conner, Liz Cohen, the Civic Center "Heart of the City" Farmers' Market, Cell Space, Chris Carlsson, the cable-car gripman who rang his bell in time with the striking hotel workers on Powell Street, Gray Brechin, Cheryl Barton, Alli Starr and Art and Revolution, Dennis Adams, and the abandoned dentist's office above K&T Erotic Books where Susan had her first San Francisco exhibition in 1974.

DATE DUE

HIGHSMITH #45115